Social Bonds to City Hall

Social Bonds to City Hall

How Appointed Managers Enter, Experience,
and Leave Their Jobs in Western Local Government

edited by
Peter Dahler-Larsen

ODENSE UNIVERSITY PRESS
2002

© The authors and Odense University Press 2002
Printed by Narayana Press
ISBN 87-7838-617-9
Cover design by Unisats ApS
Cover Illustration: Inge Lise Westman
Published with support from University of Southern Denmark.
Recommended for publication by Professor Dr. Poul Erik Mouritzen, Professor Kurt Klaudi Klausen, Ph.D. and Associate Professor Søren Winter.

Odense University Press
Campusvej 55
DK-5230 Odense M
Phone: +45 6615 7999
Fax: +45 6615 8126
E-mail: Press@forlag.sdu.dk
Internet: www.oup.dk

Distribution in the United States and Canada:
International Specialized Book Services
5804 NE Hassalo Street
Portland, OR 97213-3644 USA
Phone: +1-800-944-6190

Contents

Foreword 7

Preface 8

**CEOs and Their Bonds to City Hall
– a Thematic and Methodological Introduction** 9

Chapter 1
**The Glass Cage: the Institutional Structure
Around the Position of Municipal CEO** 21

Chapter 2
Changes in Required Qualifications for CEOs: an Analysis of Job Postings . . 30

Chapter 3
Background and Recruitment Characteristics of European CEOs 45

Chapter 4
**Beyond the City Hall: Municipal Administrative Leadership
and Local Community** 51

Chapter 5
**Values of Local Government CEOs in Job Motivation:
How Do CEOs See the Ideal Job?** 57

Chapter 6
**Playing by the Rules in Portuguese Local Government:
Interpretations of the Discourse of Administrative Leadership** 76

Chapter 7
Actors, Structures, and Rules: the Life of Danish CEOs 89

Chapter 8
**Threats and Challenges in the Organizational Environment
Affecting the CEO** 101

Chapter 9
Leaving the Job as CEO 117

Methodological Appendix 137

Participants in the U.Di.T.E. Leadership Study 146

References 148

Foreword

This book is a testament to the value of collaboration. It is based on the unique comparative research project developed initially in cooperation with the Association of the European Local Government Chief Executives. The French acronym for this association – U.Di.T.E (Union des Dirigeants Territoriaux de L'Europe) – gave the project its name: *The U.Di.T.E. Leadership Study.* The project was extended beyond Europe and supported by the International City Management Association based in the United States and the Australian Institute for Municipal Management. The collaboration with and encouragement from the practitioners who head up the city governments in the fourteen countries was a critical contribution to the inception of the project and its success in securing the responses from over 4,000 CEOs. I and the other members of the international research group extend our warm thanks to the U.Di.T.E. board of directors, the ICMA and the AIMM and to the national associations of local government CEOs who have all recommended their members to participate in the study.

The project was coordinated by a group of committed scholars who came together to shape a common methodology, conduct research in their separate countries, and then helped to prepare the common data set for analysis. There has been a substantial investment of time and resources in joint planning and coordination to ensure high quality research, data preparation, and analysis. The project has been a model in cross-national collaboration in pursuit of common research interests.

The present volume is the second of three planned books from the U.Di.T.E. Leadership Study. The two other books are:

Klausen, K.K. & A. Magnier, eds. (1998). *The Anonymous Leader: Appointed CEOs in Western Local Government*, Odense: Odense University Press.

P.E. Mouritzen & J. Svara (2002). *Leadership at the Apex. Politicians and Administrators in Western Local Governments*. Pittsburgh: Pittsburgh University Press.

Our viewpoints have been broadened considerably by our interactions. It has been a pleasure to work so closely and smoothly with 35 colleagues from the 14 countries and I owe every one of them thanks for their excellent work and enthusiastic participation. I also wish to thank the Danish Social Science Research Council and the Local Government VAT Fund for financial support to this project.

Odense, June 2001
Poul Erik Mouritzen, coordinator of the U.Di.T.E. Leadership Study

Preface

I wish to thank Poul Erik Mouritzen for organizing the U.Di.T.E. project, Jim Svara for his highly competent help with so many aspects of this book, and Steven Sampson for his careful copy-editing of the text. In addition, Vibeke Pierson and Steffen Petersen deserve special thanks for their meticulous work with references, data, tables, and drafts. Last, but not least, I wish to thank all members of the U.Di.T.E. research team. It was a lot easier to be fascinated by this extraordinary project and the people involved in it than it was to complete a book about it.

Odense, June 2001

Peter Dahler-Larsen

CEOs and Their Bonds to City Hall
– a Thematic and Methodological Introduction

BY PETER DAHLER-LARSEN

The importance of local government in the function of modern Western states lies not only in the implementation of national policies but in our very conceptions of a democratic polity (Ben-Elia 1996). In recent years, administrative leadership of local governments has responded to the pressures generated by financial strain, control from central government, structural reforms, and demands from citizens, users and organized interests (Flynn & Strehl 1996; Ben-Elia 1996). The immense variety in the structure and tasks of local government, various historical and cultural traditions, and unique combinations of changes in each country have lead local administrative leadership to change in several ways. There is no universal convergence in the forms and structures of local government (Flynn & Strehl 1996, 4). Yet some tendencies, such as the upgrading of the educational background of administrative leaders, seem to be quite generalized. Moreover, what in many countries used to be a safe life-long employment in public administration has increasingly become either a short step in one's career plan or a stressful job characterized by cross-pressures and the risk of being fired.

This book is about the bonds between individual CEOs and their organization in Western local governments. At first glance, this 'bond' is rather unequivocal: you either have the job or you don't. On closer examination, however, we observe that the legal, monetary and other terms of the formal 'contract' between the CEO and his/her organization vary greatly depending on the institutional context in which the position of the CEO is embedded. (The political climate affects the bond as well, see Svara & Mouritzen 2001). In addition, the bond is not only defined by the regulative dimensions of salaries, rights, obligations, rules and sanctions, but also along normative and cognitive ones, as are institutional arrangements in general (Scott 1995). Our concept of a 'bond' thus includes the various normative and cultural ties which tie CEOs to their administrative organizations.

Since Etzioni's (1972) and other classical studies of organization, it has been known that a study of the nature of this bond in all its aspects illuminates the fundamental orientations and motivations of organizational members and the means by which organizations seek to influence them. The social bond between organizations and individuals is a conceptual key to organizational life and culture.

To illustrate this, consider two examples. The first is Weber's depiction of how a typical bureaucrat relates to an organization. The bureaucrat is recruited on the basis of formal qualifications and merit only. He is expected to be tied to the organization in a reciprocal way: In return for life-long tenure, the bureaucrat delivers 'faithful management' and loyalty towards the larger 'impersonal and functional purposes' of the organization. In other words, provided that no extreme violations of formal rules take place, the bureaucrat leaves office only due to natural reasons such as age. In the meantime, the bureaucrat is 'chained to his activity by his entire material and ideal existence' (Weber 1946, 228). In Weber's penetrating analysis, every detail of the bond between the individual and the administrative system, including predictable career patterns, discipline and a professionalism emphasizing emotional detachment from work, is designed to enhance a specific set of values representative of the bureaucracy in modern society, such as rationality, objectivity, neutrality, and, above all, predictability. In other words, the tie between the individual and the organization reflects values and concerns of wider cultural and institutional contexts.

As a contrasting example, consider the American city manager serving 'at the pleasure' of the city council. Although the civil service system, which contains many elements of the bureaucratic model, was well established in the early twentieth century, the proponents of the new council-manager form of government conceive the city manager as someone outside the civil service system. This official would be a 'controlled executive' who occupies an important and visible position of leadership but was removable at any time – with or without cause – by the governing board. Although persons appointed to the position were supposed to be professionally qualified, there was no restriction on the ability of the city council to appoint whomever it preferred. Similarly, although city managers were supposed to be guided in the performance of their duties by expertise, the nature and quality of management depended on the characteristics of incumbents and the influence of the political context in which they worked. In the 1970s, it was still relevant to ask whether city managers were 'professional helping hands, or political hired hands' (Stillman 1977). In addition, city managers themselves often did not expect to remain in their position for very long. They reserved the option of seeking new opportunities at their own discretion. Extensive training and experience and 'bureaucratic values' – in the positive sense of that term, and extended periods of service are common among city managers, but these characteristics result from individual choices of elected officials and administrators guided by powerful values rather than being required. This 'discretionary' model fits the Australian as well as the American experience better than the Weberian model.

In both situations, however, the form of the bond between the CEO and City Hall reflects broad cultural values and institutional practices.

These contexts of local government are undergoing change. In recent years, local governments in the Western world have been faced with a variety of demands. To varying extents, regulation has been imposed on local governments by central and regional authorities, and financial strains and demands from citizens and organized interest groups seem to be the order of the day. New ideologies and philosophies of leadership and organization, such as those under the label of New Public Management, have had various impacts under different regimes of local government. If New Public Management signifies an increased focus on results and efficiency, on flexible and responsive types of public administration, and if new theories of leadership focus on charismatic and visionary leadership (Bryman 1992), the Weberian model of the tie between the CEOs and their organizations is probably under more pressure than the discretionary model.

Yet these two models are just that – conceptual models. Additional distinctions may help us understand more about the nature of the bond between CEOs and their organizations. One such distinction is whether central government and its representatives – such as prefects in Southern European countries – are involved in the geographical distibution of CEOs in various municipalities. The so-called 'Napoleonic system', according to which central authorities decide how individual CEOs move from one municipality to another during their career, has sought to ensure the independence of the CEO from factional local interests. Although the type of employment involved here in many ways resembles the classic bureaucratic model, the role of central government in connecting particular CEOs with particular municipalities on a non-voluntary basis adds distinct features to the bond between the involved partners.

Additional characteristics of the bond could be mentioned. Empirically, we are likely to find a vast and increasing variety of patterns of recruitment and career, fixed term or practically life-long appointments, various value orientations and motivations among CEOs, etc.

Our perspective on the changing ties between appointed CEOs and local government is comparative. To our knowledge, this is the first book on this issue based on a study of 14 countries: Australia, Belgium, Denmark, Finland, France, Ireland, Italy, the Netherlands, Norway, Portugal, Spain, Sweden, United Kingdom, and the United States.

These countries are characterized by different historical traditions of local government and by diverse legal and structural frameworks defining the position of CEO of local government. Indeed, the term 'local government' covers anything from the small municipalities in rural Spain to large British cities, and stands for a wide or narrow range of functions in modern Western societies. To merely suggest the variety of its scope and range of its functions, let us mention that among the above-mentioned countries, local government spends from 4% of GDP in Portugal to 27% in Denmark (OECD 1996).

Faced with this diversity, we nevertheless found a common denominator. It is the structural equivalence of the CEOs position in the structure of government. All of the approximately 4000 persons who have answered the joint questionnaire on which the U.DiT.E. study is based are the highest administrative officials of the lowest tier of government. It is in relation to this particular position that we describe the diversity and variations in the book. We discuss variations in recruitment patterns and educational backgrounds of municipal CEOs. We explore the rich variety of values, norms, expectations, and frustrations between CEOs and their work organizations.

And we explain the reasons why the CEOs leave office, some of them due to individual career motives or to organizational pressures and conflicts.

These issues are important to both scholars and practitioners. It is a considerable scholarly challenge to understand the factors and processes which explain how particular bonds between individuals and organizations are created, maintained and dissolved over time and across nations, organizations, and individuals. As Etzioni understood in 1972, the bond between individuals and organizations is a microcosm in which the organization reveals its broad nature. In other words, this study is an opportunity to learn more about the nature of the job as a municipal CEO as well as the broad changes in the organizational and institutional setting around the job. The study of the bond between administrative leaders and their work organizations is also relevant to a number of practical issues and policy-related questions in local government. For example, what impact do structural reforms have on the job as an administrative leader in local government? What are the value orientations and educational backgrounds of the people applying for the job today? How are the required qualifications defined? What impact do pressures on local government have on CEOs? And finally, why do CEOs in some settings have long tenures, while others run the daily risk of being fired?

The Comparative Approach: Promises and Pitfalls

A few methodological remarks are pertinent before the reader is invited to explore the different chapters, each based on its own thematic and methodological approach. We shall confine ourselves to matters of methodological principles. Technical details about the different sources of data are described in the methodological appendix.

The most important data source in the study is a survey questionnaire with a joint set of questions given to municipal CEOs in Australia, Belgium, Denmark, Finland, France, Ireland, Italy, the Netherlands, Norway, Portugal, Spain, Sweden, United Kingdom, and the United States. In addition, a content analysis of job announcements was carried out in Denmark, Finland, France, the Netherlands, Norway, Sweden and the UK. In selected countries teams of researchers have carried out combinations of qualitative interviews and observation studies.

In sum, we have several sources of data, 14 different countries, and two levels of data (the country level and the individual/municipality level).

Ragin (1994) distinguishes broadly between three types of methods: qualitative methods, comparative methods, and quantitative methods. In his categorization, qualitative methods are used to study commonalities among a set of phenomena. Comparative methods are used to explain diversity within a set of cases. Finally, quantitive methods are used to identify relations between variables in large populations.

Although data describing different countries often lend themselves to comparative analysis, this is only one among several possible approaches. Cross-national comparison is not, per se, a superior methodological approach to, say, the qualitative approach. It depends on the research question. If we want to know, for instance, whether the ideas of New Public Management have influenced CEOs in Western democracies, or whether we have seen a general educational upgrading among them recently, we would ask questions about potential, broad commonalities among the CEOs. More often than not, it is wise to describe the status of the population in toto before we analyze differences among segments of it.

In addition, it may be fruitful to describe situations in each individual country in depth. Sometimes such a case study may be of intrinsic value (Stake 1994), sometimes it is of instrumental value as a necessary stepping stone towards a genuine comparative analysis.

Much can be said in support of descriptive, qualitative analyses, especially in relation to the exploratory moments of research. We are in the exploratory mode more often than we think. A study like the present one – of CEOs in 14 different countries – is to a large extent exploratory. Chapters with a descriptive, qualitative intent therefore have a justification in themselves.

Yet to account for differences among countries, we turn to comparative analysis. Why do some countries offer their CEOs life-long employment while others do not? Why do CEOs leave their job for such different reasons in different countries?

Methodological problems in comparative analysis are long-standing issues in studies of political and administrative systems. Although no attempt is made here to provide a full overview over these issues, it is fair and useful to share with the reader the methodological questions which we found most pressing during the research process.

One of the most fundamental questions in comparative analysis is whether the unit of analysis is really the same across the cases studied. To reiterate, our basic unit of analysis (the highest administrative official in the lowest tier of government) is *structurally equivalent* across countries. However, it is not functionally equivalent. Local government has different areas of responsibility in different political systems. Furthermore, small rural municipalities are different from large American cities in almost all aspects of their organization. Evidently, there are also considerable semantic differences. Some refer to our objects of analysis as 'city', 'city hall' and 'city manager.' As the project evolved, we found that 'municipality' and 'CEO' gained ground. However, these terms often do not match the emic terms used in each nation. Some authors have good substantial reasons to write about 'CAOs' or 'city managers' rather than CEOs. Where this is the case, the terminology preferred by each author has been maintained in the text. The terms 'municipality' and 'municipal CEO' remain the most frequently used terms.

Another debatable point is whether it is appropriate to aggregate the individual data to the country level as it is done in this and in many other comparative analyses. 'Country' is a proxy for a specific pattern of culture, language, and institutions. But in many respects, the same is true for regions. Nevertheless, the 14 countries remain in focus in the comparative analyses in this book.

Another key concern in comparative analysis is whether a particular variable, factor or question means the same across countries (and across languages and cultures). Translations of the joint questionnaire were made from Danish into English, and from English into the language of each country. Translations both transfer and transform meanings. Is *'lavoro'* in Italian best translated into 'work' or 'job'? A rough distinction between differences in semantics and differences in substance may help us avoid the most serious mistakes in cross-cultural interpretations. When questions of interpretation are more complex, however, the distinction between the two cannot be maintained (Tompkins 1987). *'What we may take as the 'measurement core' of a variable is embedded in a social structure and a culture that give the measure a different meaning'* (Rokkan *et al.* 1969, 78).

Apparently simple measures such as years of education have very different implications in different societies. In addition, when CEOs offer 'political advice' to their mayor, the very term 'political' may carry semantic connotations that are both symbolic and substantial at the same time. Furthermore, as suggested by a classical distinction between 'emic' and 'etic' perspectives in qualitative studies, the meanings attached to a term by insiders and outsiders, respectively, in this case by CEOs and researchers, may differ (Denzin & Lincoln 1994). Until such issues are addressed, the most sophisticated techniques for analyzing comparative data will remain epistemologically unsophisticated (Mackie & Marsh 1995, 187).

The comparability of scores on variables across countries is also complicated by the fact that respondents in different countries are likely to use questionnaire scales in different ways.

For some countries information on certain variables is missing. Missing data may be randomly distributed, but are often systematically distributed according to certain institutional and cultural characteristics. In some countries, certain questions were eliminated because national researchers felt that these questions would reduce the response rate and/or lead to invalid answers. Missing data are thus not only 'missing'. The fact that they are missing is itself significant. For example, job announcements exist only in countries having an open labour market for CEOs.

Finally, it is sometimes difficult to determine the status of a particular country in relation to a particular variable. Reforms of the municipal system have been carried out in several, if not most of the countries in the U.Di.T.E study. Some structural elements are changed overnight, while other elements of old structures survive for decades as integrated parts of new structures. The same country is not really 'the same' at different times (Lijphart 1971, 689), but has it as of today changed enough to satisfy our criteria for a specific characterization? Our comparative analysis sometimes requires not only categorizations of different phenomena, but different phenomena undergoing change.

To gauge the dimension of these problems, and to partly compensate for them, we have found it helpful to engage in intense dialogues between researchers from different countries, thus pooling our knowledge. The fact that we could triangulate between different sources of data has also been valuable. Taken together, job postings and survey data tell a story about what it means to be a CEO that none of these data sources could tell by themselves.

Yet at the end of the day, the core of the comparative logic is an ambition to *account for differences*. For example: why is it that in Belgium, CEOs tend to stay in office longer than in any other country in Europe? Is it because pressure from citizens and organized interest groups is less than in other countries? Or is it due to institutionalized rules and career patterns, for instance, the fact that many CEOs in Belgium with an internal career and internal educational background get stuck in small cities and only those with a university degree can apply for a few jobs in the large cities?

In other words, to build up potential explanations that are valid across nations, we first *need knowledge about the individual case which is as deep as it would have been had we first carried out a qualitative analysis of it.* And to compare Belgium to another country with a similar relevant variable, we need an equal amount of knowledge about that country.

In this sense, qualitative analysis can be seen as a basic precondition on which to base other approaches such as the comparative one. Regrettably, we researchers run into limitations in our specific knowledge about other countries. Individual researchers rarely possess all relevant knowledge about all the cases. In addition, the criteria for relevance develop along with the comparative research process itself (Ragin 1994, 114).

Here again, the interchange of information between the national teams of researchers has been extremely valuable. Country reports (Klausen & Magnier 1998) and informal communication have triggered the necessary learning processes. For example, an initial search for explanatory variables in the number of CEOs leaving office due to career concerns could not make sense of Italy's high score on this variable. When the Italian researcher explained the functioning of the so-called 'Napoleonic system', according to which central government influences the geographical dispersion of CEOs over time according to a larger plan, the futility of premature attempts to identify correlations was obvious.

Yet our ambition in a comparative study is not only to understand the case of *the other* country, such as Belgium and Italy. Our ambition is sometimes to construct *explanations* with reference to more general principles. We want to identify a regularity which accounts for variations in phenomena of interest across cases.

In Przeworski's and Teune's (1970) terminology, *the ambition of the comparative method is thus, in brief, to eliminate proper names.* Instead, we identify regularities which hold across cases. Rather than talking about 'Belgium' or 'the Italian factor', we should gradually attempt to see in these countries merely specific constellations of more general explanatory principles.

Ragin (1994) emphasizes the gradual, and sometimes difficult, nature of this process. While some argue that the comparative and the statistical method are simply two aspects of a single method (the difference depending only on the number of cases (Lijphart 1971, 684)), Ragin insists that what distinguishes the comparative method from the statistical one is precisely the in-depth interest in the specific *constellations of factors* in each country rather than immediate sweeping statistical generalizations. These 'constellations' are functionally interdependent phenomena which tend to cluster together in 'syndromes' within each country (Przeworski & Teune 1970).

This process requires considerable attention. And there is often no perfect solution. Given a relatively small number of cases, which is typical for the comparative method, there is typically several differences between countries which are compared. Thus, the dependent phenomenon is often 'over-determined' (Lijphart 1975, 172). The situation in which one is certain that two societies are identical in all respects save one is extremely rare, if not impossible (Lijphart 1971, 688). Thus, we are reminded, that 'comparability is a quality that is not inherent in any given set of objects; rather it is a quality imparted to them by the observer's perspective' (Rustow 1968, 45-47).

Ragin suggests that we should compare configurations of phenomena. One causal factor may play different roles in its present and its absent condition, depending on the whole configuration case by case (Ragin 1994, 118). It is possible to identify complex patterns of difference – 'how different causes combine in complex and sometimes contradictory ways to produce different outcomes' (Ragin 1994, 138). These would be missed by simply 'eyeballing' the cases (ibid., 118). It is not implied here that this is what quantitative analysts do. However, Ragin is correct in insisting on the distinct identity of the comparative method. The difference between quantitative analysis and comparative method rests not only on the number of cases.

As Stake (1994) points out, however, researchers often jump too quickly from the complex particularities of a case to the few characteristics of a case which make it comparable to other cases. In a similar vein, one often jumps too quickly from a comparative analysis to a rough, quantitative one, 'eyeballing' something which resembles a regression line on a scattergram, thereby missing subtleties in the configuration of each case.

Nevertheless, we have not resisted the temptation so to do so every now and then in the following chapters, especially when a dependent variable is nicely correlated with a good candidate for an independent one. Yet as described in any basic textbook in the methodology of social sciences, the plausibility of a causal interpretation of a correlation between any two variables depends on whether a potential third variable can explain variations in both of them. In most analyses presented in this book, it is difficult to exclude the possibility of such third variables. On the other hand, the plausibility of a finding is enhanced in those situations where no such obvious candidate for a control variable can be found. In any case, we think of well-explained quantitative regularities between variables as good support for particular hypotheses rather than a demonstration of the definitive truth.

At this point, it may be wise to clarify the meaning of the term 'variable.' This is especially critical because the U.Di.T.E. data in this book cover two levels: countries and individuals/municipalities. The term 'variable' is all too often thought of as an almost physical property with a fixed content. Perhaps it is more fruitful to think of a variable as a constructed name given to certain differences in certain properties among members of a population. In other words, the meaning of a variable tacitly depends on the population within which it is supposed to describe differences. This brings us to the issue of analysis of multi-level data. Following Hofstede, Bond and Luk (1993), four types of analyses of multi-level data can be sorted out:

1. The pancultural analysis, pooling the data from all individuals (or municipalities here), regardless of the culture to which they belong.
2. A within-culture analysis, limited to each culture in the study.
3. An ecological analysis of differences between cultures. Each culture may be represented by aggregate measures of the variables for each individual (or municipality) in the culture.[1]
4. An individual analysis performed on all individuals after elimination of the culture-level effects.

Of these four types of analysis, only 3 and 4 are entirely separate and non-overlapping. The relation between two variables is often of different nature at different levels of analysis. A positive relationship between two variables in an ecological analysis may be negative or non-existent in an individual analysis (Hofstede *et al.* 1993, 487). For example, on an organization-to-organization basis, there exists virtually no link between the content of job as a CEO and the content of the job announcement for the same job. At the country level, or 'ecological level' in the phraseology of comparative analysis, such relation exists. This lends itself to an institutional interpretation rather than one focusing on job announcements as effective pieces of communication about contingencies of the individual job. In other words, the meaning of a variable depends very much on the level of analysis which in turn hinges on the overall logic of the analysis. The whole *interpretation of the variables and the link between them shifts when the level of analysis is changed.* For this reason, *an international study is fundamentally different from replications of a national study.* We are not merely testing whether what we know to be true in Denmark is also true in Europe.

There is no absolutely correct level of analysis. It depends on the questions asked and the conceptual framework around a particular research question. The level of

---

[1] If so, we eliminate the uncertainty resulting from odd individual answers which may be a key weakness in comparative studies where N is low. The average for each country is very stable because it is based on as many data points as there are individual respondents in each country, often several hundred (Hofstede, Bond & Luk 1993, 491).

analysis reflects the theoretical standpoint of the observer (Eulau 1969, 11). In most situations in this book, the search for regularities takes the form of theorizing about differences between countries. For this purpose, we use aggregate measures of the survey data (or country characteristics such as institutional rules) describing *countries*. When we apply any other of the four types of analysis mentioned, we shall be careful to inform the reader.

Our final note concerns how much the perspective of the researcher means for the production of research results. This is sometimes due to ethnocentric biases of particular researchers who tend to view their own cultural assumptions as universally valid, a phenomenon abundantly exemplified in any critical history of comparative studies (Wiarda 1990).

The increased awareness of the perspective of the researcher is but a reflection of wider concerns in the methodology of social science. There is increasing scepticism about the ambition of finding regularities which hold over time and space, and increased search for models to describe the context-bound and changing 'regularities' (Palumbo 1985). Important works such as Clifford and Marcus (1986), Denzin and Lincoln (1994) as well as Morgan (1986), suggest that the representations researchers produce of reality – including the regularities found – are coloured by the particular vocabulary in which a researcher expresses himself or herself, a vocabulary which is in turn embedded in a particular disciplinary definition and a cultural, historical, and institutional context of the research. Organizational theories are culture-bound (Hofstede 1996). Yet the displays of diversity and variety produced by the comparative method may also be exactly those factors which 'force observers to escape from ethnocentrism' (Mackie & Marsh 1995, 174).

Sometimes there is a simple and not illegitimate reason why researchers produce different results when the same set of data is made available for them. Applying different perspectives, they are quite simply not interested in asking the same questions to the data.

Reflecting, in retrospect, on the methodological dimension of the vast U.Di.T.E. project, we could have intensified our efforts in certain areas. We would like to have had even more time to engage in theoretical dialogues between the involved researchers. We would have preferred to integrate the findings from the qualitative interviews more directly into these dialogues. And we would have liked to know more about each individual country, so as to know more exactly when it is appropriate to replace a proper name of a country by a given set of variables – the classical ambition of the comparative method – and especially when it is still too early to take this step. Yet at a certain point, every project has its limits.

In the following chapters, each author asks specific questions and answers them using various methodological approaches. The participating authors represent six different countries and diverse epistemological traditions. The reader is invited to explore the resulting variety of the images of the ties between municipal CEOs and their organizations presented in this book. No strict, common methodological grid has been imposed. The editorial strategy is to allow each chapter to explore the fruitfulness of its own approach. This implies that the sample of countries dealt with in each chapter varies from one to a few to all fourteen.[2]

Yet the chapters are interconnected in many ways. As the description of the bond between CEOs and their organizations unfolds through the chapters, each contribution describes an aspect of the bond which is subsequently described again, then from a different perspective.

Outline of the Book

The chapters are organized according to a logical flow, beginning with the creation of the individual-organizational bond, followed by the various aspects of this bond, and finally, by the factors leading to its dissolution. In chapter 1, Yves Plees and Kristof de Leemans describe the structural and legal frameworks for the position as CEO in Western local government. They present a broad historical overview of the structural reforms in different countries. These structural reforms include decentralization and amalgamations. These processes affect the size of municipalities and influence the nature and content of the job as a CEO. The authors also cover the key dimensions in the various institutional set-ups which define the formal requirements and career opportunities for CEOs. Procedures for hiring and firing, formal rules and requirements as well as historical traditions are all ingredients in the formation of particular bonds between CEOs and their organizations. This preliminary analysis of the organizational machinery in which CEOs function is the necessary basis for the further inquiry into the nature of the tie between CEOs and their organizations in this volume.

The communication of required qualifications in job announcements for municipal CEOs is the subject of Chapter 2, by Peter Dahler-Larsen. Considerable changes in the required qualifications have taken place, leading to an increased focus on the personal characteristics of the leaders and reflecting the norms and values of New Public Management, such as a business-oriented and result-oriented approach to work. The analysis shows that 'qualifications' are based on a considerable element of social construction, because the content of the job announcements reflects time- and country-specific patterns and is sometimes better explained by the participation of consultants in the search process than by the actual job content.

In Chapter 3, Irene Delgado, Lourdes Nieto and Eliseo López analyse the characteristics of the CEOs in their present positions such as social background, age, gender, and educational background.

Annick Magnier describes in Chapter 4 the career patterns of the CEOs. The degree of localism in these patterns is described.

---

[2] If the main theme of a chapter concerns the difference between Northern and Southern Europe, Australia and the US may be exempt from the analysis etc.

In Chapter 5, Mikael Søndergaard describes CEOs' work goals and values. Do the work goals of municipal CEOs reflect larger cultural patterns as captured in Hofstede's cultural dimensions, i.e. individualism, masculinity, uncertainty avoidance, and power distance? And how do the work goals of the CEOs differ from comparable samples of managers in the private sector?

Chapter 6, by José Pinheiro Neves and Joel Felizes, and Chapter 7, by Morten Balle Hansen, provide ethnographically oriented 'thick descriptions' based on interviews and observations of how municipal CEOs are connected to their jobs in Portugal and Denmark. These two countries stand for the highest and the lowest score among the fourteen countries with respect to local government's expenditure of GDP. They also exemplify the often-used categories of 'Northern' and 'Southern' Europe and are located at different places in Hofstede's cultural world maps. But what lies behind Hofstede's dimensions? Chapters 6 and 7 each open a door to concrete social practices which are often viewed as a black box in quantitative analyses. The chapters enrich our understanding of the complex and multi-faceted nature of the social bond between CEOs and their jobs.

Chapter 8 returns us to the broad international overview when Andy Asquith analyzes the pressures in the organizational environment which CEOs feel have a direct impact on their job. These pressures involve control from upper-level government and financial strain, political conflict in the municipality, and political demands and pressures from citizens, organized interests, etc.

In the final chapter, Niels Ejersbo and Peter Dahler-Larsen explain why some CEOs stay in office for a long time while others leave. With some variation, the general trend is that the classical bureaucratic model of life-long employment in the same organization has decreased. The chapter analyses two types of reasons for leaving office: career motives, i.e. the CEO leaves office in order to find a better job elsewhere, and cooperation problems, i.e. when the CEO resigns or is asked to resign due to conflicts with the mayor, with politicians in the council or with other administrators. The chapter demonstrates that only a complex interplay between country-specific and organization-specific factors can explain the dynamics of CEOs leaving office.

CHAPTER 1

The Glass Cage: the Institutional Structure Around the Position of Municipal CEO

BY YVES PLEES AND KRISTOF DE LEEMANS

Introduction

The CEO does not operate in a vacuum. The CEO's work is conditioned by the institutional and political framework of local government, which might limit or strengthen him in his daily work, but which is all too often ignored in analysis (Stewart 1988). Moreover, this framework does not stand on its own: it is constantly recreated, and has recently come under great pressure in a number of countries. Some countries have witnessed a general public discontent with the quality of public services, a diminished legitimacy of governmental actions, more acute problems with which governments have to deal and, as a reaction to all this, a reform of institutional structures and new methods of management. This chapter deals with the institutional arrangements influencing the CEO and the municipal machinery surrounding this position.

We begin with a brief explanation of the position of the CEO in the municipal structure, followed by an assessment of the institutional and social challenges facing the CEO.

Institutional Arrangements

The Position of Local Authorities within the Framework of the State
Before discussing institutional arrangements affecting the CEO in local government, it is necessary to clarify the terms 'local government' and 'CEO'. In the context of this chapter, we will look mainly at the municipalities when discussing local authorities. With the term 'Chief Executive Officer', we denote in this context 'the highest appointed administrative official'.

Evidently, the first limiting factor for the CEO is the limits of the municipality where he/she works. Even a strong CEO, with considerable influence in his own municipality, will be severely restrained if his municipality has only limited tasks in the general framework of the state or is bound by strict regulations or instructions from higher tiers of government. Therefore, it is necessary to start by examining the position of the local government within the state system. A distinction may be made between different types of local government, each with a distinct role and position for the local authorities in the state structure and a different rationale behind it (Goldsmith, in King & Stoker 1996; Page 1990). Yet while scholars agree on the existence of different groups of local authorities, there is little agreement on how to make a classification or on the criteria for classifying countries. Some authors (Norton 1994, 40) distinguish a Northern and Southern group, a Pacific group (the US, Canada, Japan) and a European Island group (the UK, Ireland). Others (Goldsmith 1996) following Hesse and Sharpe, distinguish three groups: Anglo, North and Middle European, and a South European group. Hesse and Sharpe classify Belgium in the Southern group, Norton in the Northern group.

The difference in classification for Belgium clearly demonstrates the importance of the criteria used: when looking at the number of inhabitants (which would be an indicator of scale and thus efficiency), Belgium clearly belongs to the Northern group. If the focus is on community identification, the country also scores high: Belgium is characterised by an extremely high localism of its population and a high level of identification of the inhabitants with their municipality. This is the criterion used by Hesse and Sharpe to describe the Southern group.

Since it is already possible to discern different patterns of local government just by looking at a simple criterion such as size or community orientation, it should not be surprising that in the area of human resource management, striking differences can be found with respect to legal stipulations concerning the CEO. Moreover, looking at the internal organisation of the municipal services can be helpful in making a general classification of the municipalities. In this chapter, we will divide the countries of the U.Di.T.E. study into three groups: a North European, a South European and an Anglo group.

North European
Compared to the municipalities in the south of Europe, the North European municipalities are characterised by a larger number of inhabitants and an underlying emphasis on efficiency. They are also characterised by general competencies, the most basic of which is the idea of local self-government. Thus, there exists a strict division of powers between the different tiers of government. We can call this a 'split hierarchy' or a relatively 'autonomous municipality'. Countries in this group are: Norway, Sweden, Denmark, Finland, and the Netherlands.

South European
Municipalities belonging to the South group are not only smaller in terms of inhabitants, they also put more emphasis on localism, or community values. Their position in the framework of the state is constitutionally guaranteed, yet the powers exercized by these municipalities differ from country to country and are generally relatively limited. While the municipalities usually have general competencies, these are limited by

their small size – and thus financially dependent on higher levels of government. Municipalities from countries in this group usually have a relatively high degree of supervision from higher levels of government. This is not only true of their policies, but also in determining the position of their employees. We can call this group the 'fused hierarchy' group, where powers between levels of government are fused.

Since the municipalities are (relatively) small and weak, a number of other authorities are active in their territory: field administration from regional, state or federal level, or they cooperate individually or jointly with powerful private sector utility companies for their service delivery. We could call the municipalities in this group 'oppressed municipalities', and they are found in Portugal, Spain, France, Italy and Belgium.

Anglo Group
Characteristic for this group are the *ultra vires* principle and the pragmatic and instrumental tradition of government, which tends to see public interest as no more than the sum of private interests. Thus, local government is considered primarily as a service provider, either in its own right, or as an agent of the centre (Jones & Travers 1996). This is also reflected in the fact that local authorities are large enough for optimal service provision but not for citizen participation. The result is that as the need for services changes over time, the position of local government within the state structure also changes. Local government is at the mercy of the central level. We could characterise the municipalities in this group as 'dependent' municipalities. This is reflected in the frequent changes of competencies of local authorities. The same argument applies to the extensive use of QUANGOs.

Changes to the Framework: Amalgamations
Virtually all countries in the U.Di.T.E. study have undergone one or more series of amalgamations. Table 1.1 shows the reduction in absolute figures, in percentage, and scale enlargement index (number of municipalities in year of reference divided by number of municipalities in the year studied) as proposed by Bours (1993).

Table 1.1: Number of municipalities of countries in the U.Di.T.E. study.

Country	1950	1992	Evolution	Scale enlargement index
Sweden	2281	286	-87%	7.9
Denmark	1387	275	-80%	5.0
Belgium	2669	589	-78%	4.5
United Kingdom	2082	484	-76%	4.3
Norway	744	439	-41%	1.7
The Netherlands	1015	647	-36%	1.6
Finland	547	455	-16%	1.2
Spain	9214	8082	-12%	1.1
France	38814	36763	-5%	1.06
Portugal	303	305	0.007	.99
Italy	7781	8100	0.04	.96

In this respect, it is striking that, as Sharpe (1966) points out, the amalgamations have been more important in those countries which did not belong to the Napoleonic tradition, i.e. in the Northern and Anglo groups. Several explanations can be noted:

- Interference by the admininistration of a higher level government is relatively more important in countries with a Napoleonic tradition. This makes the role of municipalities as service providers less important in the entire institutional framework, thus decreasing the pressure for efficiency and economies of scale.
- Moreover, in a number of countries belonging to the Napoleonic group the mayors/local elite have easy access to the central level by various mechanisms, such as the *cumul des mandats* (several political roles for the same person). This, of course, is instrumental for them to avoid amalgamation, and thus, the abolition of their municipalities.

Changes to the Framework: the Rise of the Meso Level
This does not mean, however, that in the municipalities of the Southern group nothing has changed. While the number of municipalities has remained relatively stable in these countries, a completely new level of government has been introduced. The rise of the meso level is more prominent in countries with a Napoleonic tradition. Since the 1950s, we have seen the creation of new tiers of government in Spain (regions/autonomous regions), Belgium (regions/language communities), France (regions), and Italy (regions). While part of the creation of new levels of government is due to nationalist movements, the previously mentioned explanation for the amalgamations – pressure for efficiency – might also be partially applicable here, as Sharpe (1993) points out.

The fused hierarchical system which characterises the Napoleonic countries certainly has thus become more complex. It means that the local government CEO might find himself confronted with regulations and instructions coming from different levels of government. Moreover, not only do municipalities have to deal with more actors, but some of these might want to assert themselves very strongly, not against the 'higher' national or federal level, but especially towards the local authorities.

Changes to the Framework: Europe
The institutional world at the level immediately above the CEO is changing. However, this is not the only level where changes are taking place. It is also the case from the highest level: the European Union. Especially in the sphere of its regional policy, European legislation can have considerable impact on municipalities and the way they operate. Moreover, EU policies on competition mean that for public infrastructure above a certain level, tendering must be carried out at the European level.

Depending on the type of municipality and the changes it is undergoing, the position of the CEO will be different. Taking into consideration the position of the municipality itself, we could expect more powerful CEOs in the Northern group.

Municipalities in this group are stronger and more autonomous from the state. Yet this picture does not help us understand the position of the CEO within the municipality itself.

Typology of Careers

Having given a description of the 'border' which constitutes the municipality itself, we now proceed to the internal part of the municipal machinery and its constraints.

Differences in the positions at the local level are reflected in the staffing regulations. The local level in the North European group is more independent from the central level and seems to be regarded as more 'mature' than its South European counterpart. The question then remains whether this has any impact on the recruitment policies, formal qualifications required and the legal protection the CEOs enjoy.

We will now examine the following elements:

– The CEO as statutory versus contractual agent
– The requirements to become a CEO
– Hiring and firing procedures

Statutory Position Versus Contract
Looking at the staff of the municipalities (or government in general), it is possible to distinguish two ideal types of municipal agents. On one side of the spectrum is the contractual agent, whose position in terms of tasks, benefits and liabilities is governed by a contract between him and the authority. This contract can be standard or negotiated, for a fixed or indeterminate period.

On the other side of the spectrum are municipal agents whose position is governed by a statute. Yet this statute can be regulated by different levels of government, including the local authority in question. Being statutory means that by entering the service, the civil servant finds a ready-made position, which he fills and which also predetermines his future career path, salary and responsibilities: a whole career has been already planned.

If the statute is centrally decided, it indicates a weaker position of the municipalities. Indeed, if there is a centrally determined – uniform – statute for their members of staff, it places limits on the hiring power, one of the core elements of a municipality-regulated HRM policy.

Following our earlier discussion on different types of local government, we would expect the Southern group to place much more emphasis on legality, more central government supervision and even regulation, also in the field of recruitment of staff. All other things being equal, at the aggregate level this would lead to more uniformity in terms of characteristics and/or career paths. A statute usually determines not only the career, but also entrance requirements and possibly rules on promotion (this can be both in terms of job content or financial benefits). It is usually very difficult to break the contract of a statutory civil servant, this in line with Weber's principles of lifetime employment in exchange for total loyalty to the administrative system. Despite the fact that lifetime employment does not necessarily mean the same job, only rarely is a CEO put 'aside'. This tends to strengthen his position vis-à-vis the local political level.

It is quite striking that in a number of countries, the position of the CEO is statutorily determined at the local level. This indicates a relatively weak position of the municipalities. Yet even the statutory position of the municipal civil servants seems not to be the most strict framework. In a number of countries, notably Italy and Portugal, all or part of the CEOs are civil servants at the national level. This may be considered a further limitation upon municipal discretion, as the CEOs may act as a kind of local watchdog on behalf of the national level. Even in countries where the CEO is a municipal agent, he still can be considered a kind of watchdog: in Belgium, for instance, he is supposed to countersign all municipal acts, but to refuse his signature if the acts are illegal. Note, however, that he cannot refuse his signature for reasons other than illegality.

Summing up, it should not surprise us that such a statutory position of the CEO can be found in countries belonging to the Southern group: Portugal, Italy, (national civil servants), Spain and Belgium.

The Northern group in this hypothesis would thus be characterised by more freedom in terms of regulations, competencies, hiring/firing strategies etc., or in other terms, with more opportunities to use the external labour market. This does not mean, however, that municipalities in this group *will* use more external labour markets: indeed, some authors point to the advantage of an internal labour market in terms of keeping valued workers or reducing staff turnover, thus avoiding costs of selecting new staff (Wise 1996).

In principle, the contractual hiring offers much more freedom to the local authorities, especially if their contracts give them a free hand with regard to qualifications and duration of contract. It gives the municipalities the freedom to specify the profile of the CEO according to their own needs or wishes. This can go even as far as deciding not to have a CEO at all.

Moreover, in most cases the contract is for only a fixed number of years, leaving the municipalities to pay the cost of either negotiating again with the present CEO or finding another suitable candidate when the contract expires. On the other hand, the contract provides a strong incentive (or forces the municipality) to check the performance of the CEO and, if necessary, to find another.

Between countries, or even within countries, a wide variety of practices can still be found: in some countries municipalities can themselves decide the duration of a contract, in other countries, such as Norway, the national level decides the duration of a position. In some countries, a certain range of possible salaries and other contractual elements of the job are predefined and thus not negotiable.

Thus, a contract does not necessarily allow a maximum degree of freedom to a municipality: the Irish local level, as Asquith and O'Halpin stress, is not free to decide which particular person becomes their CEO.

Generally, municipalities which best fit the model of a CEO as a contractual agent are found in the North European and Anglo groups.

Qualifications

Both the statute and the contract may specify certain, required qualifications. These may take the form of a minimum age (maturity), professional experience in terms of seniority, a university degree or additional qualifications.

It is not uncommon for qualifications to differ according to the size or other specific characteristics of the municipality. Especially size, in terms of number of inhabitants, seems to be a very powerful determinant of education of the CEO. In this respect, amalgamations can have a serious impact on the job prospect of would-be CEOs.

Of course, qualifications are not only linked to the size of the municipality, but also to the job: depending on the job content, the CEO needs to be qualified. The fact that CEOs in the Southern group quite often have this 'controlling' function on behalf of other levels of government could also mean that they are relatively better qualified than the size of municipality would suggest. In the countries of the Southern group, the central authorities determine to a considerable degree the qualifications needed for a candidate CEO.

In general, however, there is no guarantee that the institutionally (statutory or contractual) required qualifications will perfectly match the actual content of the job.

Hiring and Firing

Closely linked to the required qualifications are the hiring procedures. Here again there is a difference between the contractual and statutory CEO. Statutory CEOs often have to pass an exam. This exam can be for the particular vacancy (Belgium) or it may be a more general public sector exam, independent of a vacancy (Italy, Spain). The hiring of a contractual CEO is sometimes carried out by the municipality, mostly the council (Netherlands), sometimes the mayor (France), and sometimes by an independent board (UK, Ireland).

Among the different means of ending the relationship between the employee and the employer, the most common is the expiration of the contract and retirement. However, it is sometimes a question of dismissal. Here the legal position of the statutory civil servant usually gives more protection than the contract, which even might have certain provisions for these cases.

The different views of local authorities in different countries lead to differences in staff regulations, as table 1.2 shows:

Table 1.2: CEO contractual and tenure provisions among U.Di.T.E. countries.

Country	Contract /statute	Predetermined time
Belgium	S	Y: life
Finland	C	N: council decides itself, can be for life
Italy	S	Y: life
Ireland	C	N: appointment. Com. decides
Spain	S	Y: life
Portugal	C	Y: 3 years
Denmark	C	Y: authority decides
Sweden	C	Y/N: authority decides
Norway	C	Y: six years
The Netherlands	C	Y/N: council decides
France	C	N: depends on mayor
UK	C	N

Table 1.2 again demonstrates the North – South division noted earlier. The municipalities in the Southern group clearly lack the freedom typical for members of the Northern group in deciding the terms of employment and remuneration.

Challenges to the CEO

Within this framework, the CEO has a number of battles to fight; these are unrelated to his position within the municipal framework and independent of his statute or type of contract. Yet the position of the CEO within the municipal framework, and the strength of the municipality, clearly influence how the CEO will respond to various problems:

1. The *increasing discontent of citizens* with governmental actions, or in other words, the loss of legitimacy of government (Bouckaert, Hondeghem & Maes 1994, 31). Of course, the level of citizen discontent may vary from country to country, or even between regions. In a number of countries, more and more citizens feel discontented – and voice their discontent – with the inability of government to solve a number of problems which immediately affect their lives. Local bureaucracies sometimes find themselves confronted with very vague or even contradictory objectives (Goodsell 1985).
2. In a number of countries, *modernisation of the administration*, coupled with the downsizing of the core administration, an increase in privatisations and governing at arms length are also on the agenda. Related to these developments is the increasing importance of citizen-involvement in a number of administrative issues, as well as the increased protection citizens enjoy (Bouckaert, Hondeghem & Maes 1994, 33). For the CEO, privatisations and governing at arms length mean

more partners to deal with, while the various procedures for citizen consultation and participation certainly complicate the working environment. In this respect, the increased emphasis on business-style management may have the undesired outcome that citizens become even more disconnected from the administrative level than before (King & Stivers 1998, 25).
3. The *creation of new tiers of government* increases the complexity of the situation with which a CEO has to deal as well as the possibility of conflicting objectives being forced upon the local authority.
4. The CEO will be affected by *amalgamations*. For a number of CEOs, amalgamation means losing their jobs. For those who remain, a completely new work situation has to be defined. This is not only the case in terms of job content, but also entails the development of a new network of contacts.

Conclusion

Although the position of the CEO is sometimes considered to be the apex of the administration, it is far from synonymous with complete freedom. Indeed, the CEO is surrounded by an institutional 'firewall', which is not always very visible if the CEO function were studied only from the perspective of one country. The CEO's powers and position are limited by his formal position within the municipality and within the framework of the state to which it belongs. If a municipality is weak, the CEO might be strong within his organisation, but will be limited in effecting change. If the position of the municipality in the state structure changes, be it through amalgamations or through the outsourcing of a number of duties, the frame of reference of the chief executive will automatically change.

The position and formal role of the CEO within the municipal framework itself very much determine his job and its attractiveness. In this respect, we not only refer to the actual job content, but also to the CEO's legal position: the CEO is a secretary for life or a contractual manager, with a position which is brought up for review every few years. All these elements create a glass cage for the CEO, a cage which is shaped differently in different countries. This becomes visible only by viewing the CEO from different perspectives, an option only offered by the comparative method.

CHAPTER 2

Changes in Required Qualifications for CEOs: an Analysis of Job Postings

BY PETER DAHLER-LARSEN

Introduction

Much has been said about changes affecting local political systems in general, such as budget restraints, control from central government, increased demands on service from citizens and organized groups, new administrative philosophies, new forms of governance, new administrative structures, and changing values. Presumably, these changes lead to changes in the job content and role of the CEO, such as more emphasis on generalized management rather than specific administrative issues, new relations to political leaders, more responsive relations to citizens, etc. Presumably, again, these changes affect the required qualifications for CEOs. Certainly, considerable changes in the educational background of CEOs can be observed. However, not much is known about the processes through which the above-mentioned changes are transformed into specific requirements for CEOs in practice. There may be many 'loose couplings', as changes in the environments of local governments are transformed into organizational changes, and, organizational changes transformed into specific requirements to CEOs. Finally, these requirements can be expressed in several ways, such as the demand for certain formal skills, the ability to perform certain functions or the possession of certain personal traits.

In many countries, these requirements are quite tightly controlled by a statute (see previous chapter), i.e. by institutional rules which define entry criteria in terms of a formal education, certificate, etc. This chapter examines the specific requirements as they appear in job postings. Per definition, variations in job requirements exist only in countries where there is some discretionary element in the definition of the CEO position (see the methodological appendix for further details). Here, we shall focus on job postings from seven of the U.Di.T.E. countries: Denmark, Finland, Norway, the Netherlands, France, Sweden and the United Kingdom. The sample is skewed. Among the Southern European countries, only France is represented.

In order not to be overwhelmed by the many dimensions of our topic, we shall provide a general overview and then focus on requirements made on the CEO as a change agent.

Theoretically, we shall be guided by two broad perspectives: (1) contingency theory, which suggests that job requirements are determined by job content which is in turn determined by internal and external contingency factors; and (2) institutional theory, which suggests that requirements are 'free floating', i.e. not based on job contents but on norms, values, and institutional carriers on the level of organizational fields.

Why Study Job Postings?

Job postings are public announcements. After publication in journals they are usually stored in libraries. This means they are available for historical analysis, which is often not the case for survey data. One of the strengths of content analysis is to display changes in the content of a particular communication channel over time (Holsti 1969). Here we focus on three points in time: 1975, 1985, and 1995.

Job postings are brief public announcements with the official purpose of attracting a qualified person to fill a vacant position. Whether or not a job posting succeeds in attracting the 'right' applicant, it presents the municipal organization in certain ways. It may persuade the municipal environment about its effectiveness. It may or may not use consultants to act as intermediary story-tellers, allowing them to say something that the municipality cannot say about itself. A job posting may target not only potential applicants, but also other municipalities in the field as well as the municipality's own employees (Broms & Gahmberg 1983). Within this multi-faceted communicative situation, a job posting is a brief public declaration of what the organization thinks it needs.

Various understandings of organizational processes give different explanations of how such a need is defined, thus leading to at least three different ideal-typical motivations for the study of job postings:

1. According to a preliminary understanding, the qualifications required for a job are a result of a number of contingency factors such as the technical tasks included in the job and the organizationally-structurally defined rights and duties involved in the position at hand. The best job posting is the one that most succinctly communicates these contingency factors in order to precisely and efficiently attract exactly the best qualified person but not many others (Dawson & Saunders 1996). In practice, however, it is quite difficult to predict which qualities lead to the best performance (Ungerson 1975, 7). It is not always easy to predict the criteria which characterize the best candidate for a job. A pencil test of office employees has been a good instrument for the selection of sharpshooting riflemen (Ungerson 1975, 7). However, other tests measuring such a relatively simple skill as the learning of the Morse alphabet have had strikingly low validity. To compensate for the considerable uncertainty involved in such prediction processes, to maintain certain myths that leadership makes a difference, and to

help distinguish between otherwise almost similar candidates for leadership positions (March 1995), a number of socially constructed definitions exist of what constitutes a good leader. As any socially constructed belief system, these definitions are rooted in social time and space. This lays the foundation for our second understanding of job postings.

2. Job postings are merely lists of socially available norms and ideas about good management. Organizations may use such lists as facades towards their environment in order to appear as legitimate actors who know how to apply 'appropriate' ideas to management. A job posting may reflect rationalized myths in the wider social setting (Meyer & Rowan 1977), but this symbolic expression may be very loosely coupled – if at all – (Weick 1976) to the job as such, and to the rest of the organization for that matter. Job postings give highly inflated and unrealistic images of what the job is about. Due to their formal and highly publicized nature and their function as images shown to the outside world, job postings provide much less accurate information about the job than more informal sources of information (Jablin 1987, 687). In this sense, job postings exemplify organizational hypocrisy (Brunsson 1986). So goes the story according to at least some versions of institutional theory.

This understanding of job postings has some limitations, however, as does any understanding of organizations based on a distinction between the 'symbolic' and the 'substantial' (Tompkins 1987). Once the 'symbolic' is there, it helps shape what can be taken as real and substantial (March & Olsen 1984). The job posting is a public document located in between what is and what is desired: it attempts to describe certain organizational realities, while also allowing ambitions for the future to be articulated. However, since it points towards the future, charlantry in the job posting may be charlantry attempting to become true. We cannot empirically determine the extent to which these attempts are purely 'symbolic.'

3. What we can do, however, – and this is our third understanding of job postings – is to analyse them as organizational discourse; as discourse job postings structure the phenomenon of municipal leadership by means of subtle rules about what can be thought and articulated (Foucault 1980; 1971). Leadership is constituted as much by what is said about it as by what is done by the holders of leadership positions (Calas & Smircich 1988, 203). We can regard job postings as a window by which these discursive formations can be shown, and we can delineate certain patterns in how the window exhibition changes over time.

Research along these lines has practical implications. Job postings are used as a source of information about the 'demands' on the labour market, and recommendations are often made about how individuals and societies should prepare for and adapt to these demands.

The Content of the Job Postings

Table 2.1 shows the growth in the number of words in the various sections of the job postings. Word frequency does not necessarily indicate importance. On the other hand, however, since the job ad is a relatively brief message, communicators must prioritize. A large growth in the number of words in any particular section indicates that the communicated messages have undergone change. Someone expects the new message to make a difference.

The average number of words in our sample of job postings increased dramatically from 1975 to 1995. Not surprisingly, the number of words concerning job content and functions has grown. This should not surprise us when we take into account the recent focus on the changing role of managing bureaucrats: they are said to become more policy-oriented, more change-oriented, more oriented towards society, less oriented towards administrative procedures, etc. It is also 'common knowledge' that these changes have made new demands on the qualifications of public managers, and in practice induced a trend towards academic upgrading. Nevertheless, the specification of formal qualifications does not require more words over the years. Instead, the discourse about personal attributes has expanded considerably. The underlying belief seems to be that the personal characteristics of public managers will make considerable differences. This is in line with recent popular understandings of good management (Bryman 1992).

Table 2.1: Number of words and the content of the job ads.

	Total		
Year	1970s	1980s	1990s
No. of words in job content and functions	15.12	20.59	44.59
No. of words in skills (formal qualifications, experience)	14.62	17.95	18.04
No. of words in personal attributes	5.46	12.67	23.76
No. of words in job benefits, salary, etc.	15.71	15.54	14.65
No. of words in municipality as area	9.13	21.88	33.51
No. of words in municipality as administrative organization	4.03	12.43	19.07
Total number of words in ad:	115.80	173.90	233.10
Number of cases:	153	192	234

Table 2.1 also indicates that the description of the municipality as an organization has expanded considerably. The marketing of the municipality as an area in the job posting has also become much more common. Our analysis thus indicates certain general tendencies:

First, there has been an *expansion of discourse on public management*. It takes up much more space than twenty years ago. To attract an applicant is no longer a matter of a simple formal announcement. It is entangled in an elaborate discourse on management.

Second, this elaboration takes place in the context of *increasing sophistication of public management*. Contrary to twenty years ago, the definition of a public management position seems to require quite more information about the organizational structures, reforms, cultures, etc., and/or other aspects of the municipal organization. Managers are expected to understand the relevance of the organizational dimensions of management and to be able to relate to, deal with, or influence these dimensions. This trend illustrates John Meyer's ideas about the general diffusion of abstract organizing ideas into specific areas of activity in the modern rationalized world (Jepperson & Meyer 1991; Strang & Meyer 1994).

Third, the changes in the ad texts reflect a *personification of management*. Many words are required to describe the desired personal profile of public managers. The personified discourse has expanded dramatically over time.

Fourth, the job ad has become a *marketing tool*. The ads devote increased emphasis to describing the municipality as an area, often by underlining whatever positive qualities may be connected to the geography, location and cultural life of the municipality. This fact, along with the increased number of words in the job ad, reflects the embedding of the discourse on management within a *marketing* context. The job posting seeks to present a marketable image of the municipality.

The Tasks and Roles of the CEOs

Some of the typical tasks in the job postings have been coded under different items which were, in turn, categorized under four main roles of top bureaucrats: civil servant, coordinator, advisor, and change agent. To compensate for coding problems, several of the roles are characterized by more than one theme.

The portrayal of managerial roles and tasks varies quite a lot over time (not shown). Some themes grow over a twenty-year period, perhaps due to the mere expansion in talk about management. Most of the themes are not mentioned at all in 1985, not to mention 1975. However, there are also themes that appear at one time and then fade. This is the case, for instance, of civil servants' role in Denmark and Sweden and of the coordinating role in Denmark, which was more emphasized in 1985 than later on. In other words, we are dealing with a moving target.

Now, let us focus on 1995 (table 2.2). The CEO's role as civil servant is strongly emphasized in France, partly in the Netherlands, and much less so in the other coun-

Changes in Required Qualifications for CEOs 35

tries. The coordinating role is underlined considerably in Sweden, France, and the Netherlands, but less so in Denmark and Norway, less in Finland, and not at all in the UK. The advisor role is much emphasized in the Netherlands, Denmark and France, less in the UK and Sweden, and not at all in Finland and Norway.

The role as a change agent is strong in the job postings in Sweden, and moderately strong in Denmark, Norway, the Netherlands and the UK in various mixtures. It is, however, strikingly weak in Finland and also in France, which scores very high on the civil servant role.

Table 2.2: The tasks of the CEOs (percentage of ads where item occurs).

Country	Denmark N=35	Finland N=25	Norway N=40	The Netherlands N=24	France N=59	Sweden N=32	UK N=19	Total N=234
Civil Servant Mean Score	*13*	*0*	*9*	*27*	*59*	*14*	*19*	*25*
Refer to political body/mayor	14	0	0	0	53	9	0	17
Implement political decisions	11	0	18	54	64	19	37	32
Coordinator Mean Score	*38*	*18*	*34*	*75*	*55*	*66*	*3*	*44*
Have cooperative skills	46	36	68	71	44	56	5	49
Coordinate branches of administration	29	0	0	79	66	75	0	39
Advisor Mean Score	*69*	*0*	*0*	*79*	*56*	*13*	*37*	*37*
Advise mayor/ political body	69	0	0	79	56	13	37	37
Change Agent Mean Score	*21*	*6*	*12*	*15*	*7*	*36*	*13*	*15*
Develop trade	26	8	3	0	12	31	0	12
Formulate goals	6	0	13	13	3	16	5	8
Formulate visions	6	0	0	4	7	25	0	6
Change/reform	3	8	3	58	2	50	32	18
Develop service	63	12	43	0	9	59	21	30

We will now analyze one aspect in more detail: the idea of the CEO as a change agent. This is a key theme in new public management. How do we account for the differences in the adoption of increasing preponderance items describing the municipal CEO as a change agent?

Does the Idea of the CEO as a Change Agent in the Job Postings Reflect the Job?

To answer this question, we compare the job posting data with survey data from the individual CEOs. We wish to go to the municipal level rather than merely the country level because if a job posting functions according to contingency theory, it emphasizes the particular characteristics of each individual job. Only on this basis can applicants be well-informed about why they should apply for this particular CEO job rather than another one in the same country.

In the survey, CEOs were asked to estimate the importance of various tasks. For five tasks, the correlation between a high ranking of a task and the occurrence of the same or very similar theme in the job posting was then checked within each country (not shown) as well as in the total population (displayed in table 2.3 below).

Due to ethical, legal, and practical limitations, this combination of data can be carried out only in Denmark, Norway, Finland and the Netherlands. The analysis is pan-cultural (see introduction) in order to achieve a sufficiently high N. Still, the normal requirements for cross-tabulation with a chi-square significance test are violated here and there in the analyses undergirding table 2.3. For the contingency perspective to be valid, however, one would have expected some positive correlations between the job posting and the content of the job. Table 2.3 displays only negative correlations.[1]

The data constitute a head-on attack on a simple contingency view of job postings as an announcement about technical tasks to be carried out. Most job posting items do not correlate with survey descriptions about the actual job. Where a correlation exists, it is negative, i.e. a particular item occurs more frequently in job postings from municipalities where the CEO reports that this task is *not* an important part of his or her daily work.

A partial explanation may be that some items are not 'appropriate' to be mentioned in a job posting, such as how important it is for the CEO to attract external resources to the municipality due to its poor economic situation. For a more general explanation, we must inquire further into the many factors that shape job postings. First, however, we will attempt to rule out another technical contingency-oriented explanation of the occurrence of the discourse of the CEO as a change agent in the job postings.

---

[1] One might argue that the total results of this pan-cultural analysis are produced by country-specific factors; for this reason, subgroups of high- and low-scoring countries on each item were also analyzed, but with similar results.

Changes in Required Qualifications for CEOs

Table 2.3: Correlation between job posting items and description of job as seen by the actual holder of job. ('Correlation' is defined as a result of a two-by-two cross-tabulation with chi^2, p <0.1).

Job postings: item occurs	Survey: item is of utmost importance or very important	Denmark, Norway, Finland and the Netherlands N=89
To formulate goals	formulate ideas and visions	negative
To formulate visions	formulate ideas and visions	no
To change/to reform	encourage new projects	no
Develop, e.g., develop service	encourage new projects	negative
Develop trade and commerce in the municipality	attract external resources	no

Does Size Matter?

Organizational size may explain the occurrence of change agent items in the job postings. Size is known to be related to so many other features of organizations; in very small administrations, there may be little to change. If the contingency version of the size argument is correct, it should be true on the organizational level, not only across countries. Now, consider table 2.4.[2]

In the Netherlands, the item change/reform occurs significantly more often in larger municipalities than in smaller ones. On the other hand, in Norway the development of services is a factor which significantly characterizes *small* municipalities. This may be due to the deliberate policy of extending infrastructure even smaller, marginal areas of this vast country. This should serve to remind us that the definition of 'tasks' for municipal CEOs has an explicit *political* dimension. Since we are dealing with the public sector, we should not over-emphasize broad 'diffusion patterns' without taking into account the ability of various political systems to define for themselves the 'tasks' that their managers have to carry out.

The table indicates that organizational size does not help us very much to explain the occurrence of the ideas of CEO as a change agent *within* countries. However, notice the results of the 'total' column in the table. Two of our five items indicating the CEO as a change agent are positively correlated to organizational size in the pan-cultural analysis. This inspires us to move the level of analysis *to that of organizational fields*.

---

[2] Here the data set is larger than in table 2.3, because we are not dependent on survey data.

Table 2.4: Correlation between CEO as a change agent and organizational size (a critical level of size is determined in each country to minimize crosstabulated cells where expected N < 5; p<=0.1).

Nation (size cut point)	Denmark (>10,000)	Finland (>10,000)	Norway (>5,000)	The Netherlands (>20,000)	France (>10,000)	Sweden (>20,000)	Total (>10,000)
N	35	25	40	24	56	32	212
Develop economy; trade; commerce	no	no	no	no	no	no	no
Formulate goals	no	no	no	no	no	no	no
Formulate visions	no	no	no	no	no	no	positive
Change/ reform	no	no	no	positive	no	no	positive
Develop, e.g., services	no	no	negative	no	no	no	no
At least one of the above	no	no	negative	positive	no	no	positive

The Effects of Organizational Size and Tasks Across Countries

We shall assume that the set of municipalities within a country can be meaningfully treated as an organizational field. An organizational field is defined in terms of degrees of structural similarity, communicative interconnections, common career patterns, etc. (DiMaggio & Powell 1991).

Table 2.5 displays the average score on the five change agent items in the job postings and the size of municipalities (measured as a percentage of municipalities above 5000 inhabitants).

On the country level, size is correlated with the occurrence of change agent items in the job postings, with the UK as a deviant case. The idea of the CEO as a change agent appears to be more easy to introduce in countries with large municipalities. This is to be expected, because one would assume that a certain 'amount' of organization and 'organizationability' is required before the idea of organizational change would appear attractive. By organizationability I mean the degree to which organizations in a field are open to a generalized understanding of management and management interventions. However, our interpretation of this (loose) relation between size and change is institutional not contingency-oriented. We have passed the individual-organization level and moved on to the norms on the country level. We sug-

Table 2.5: Mean score on change agent items in job postings compared to size of municipalities and to mean scores in survey data on the salience of various roles for CEOs country by country; ( ) = rank order.[3]

	Denmark	Finland	Norway	The Netherlands	France	UK	Sweden
Change agent (job postings)	21 (2)	6 (7)	12 (5)	15 (3)	7 (6)	13 (4)	36 (1)
Size: percentage of municipalities with above 5000 inhabitants	93 (3)	51 (5)	43 (6)	90 (4)	5 (7)	100 (1)	97 (2)
Classical bureaucrat (survey)	48 (4)	45 (7)	58 (2)	46 (6)	71 (1)	52 (3)	47 (5)

gest that size appears to matter, at least partly, because if municipalities are of a certain size within an organizational field, it makes the normative ideal of the CEO as a change agent more likely and more relevant.

We shall now examine the tasks and roles of the CEO in the same light. The average score in one of the broad roles of the CEO, i.e. the 'classical bureaucrat' is also given in table 2.5. The 'classical bureaucrat' is measured as the national mean on such items as to 'guide subordinate staff in day-to-day handling of cases', 'manage economic affairs, accounts and budgetary control', 'ensure that rules and routines are followed', and 'give the mayor legal, economic and other kinds of technical advice'.

Apart from the case of Finland, there appears to be a negative relationship between the emphasis on the two roles of classical bureaucrat versus that of change agent. In other words, *when we compare each country's set of municipalities as an organizational field, tasks and roles have an affect on discourses on management such as those found in job postings*. Once rules, norms and expectations have defined a formal role for CEOs that emphasizes the virtues of traditional bureaucracy (such as ensuring that rules and regulations are followed) this acts as a barrier towards the introduction of the CEO as a change agent. While this may be due to simple restrictions of resources (time and attention), it may also be caused by *institutionalized values and norms concerning the definition of the proper role of a CEO within each particular organizational field*. On the country level, however, the discourse on public management is not completely disconnected from tasks on the job. In other

---

[3] The CEOs were asked to indicate the relative priority of various tasks in their daily work. Each item was ranked on a five-point scale, later designated values from 0-100. The score on 'classical bureaucrat' is based on the following items: 'guide subordinate staff in day-to-day handling of cases', 'manage economic affairs, accounts and budgetary control', 'ensure that rules and routines are followed', and 'give the mayor legal, economic and other kinds of technical advice'

words, we have found that the 'demands' mentioned in the job posting from one municipality in a country are generally not correlated or even negatively correlated with tasks in the municipality, but suddenly become understandable in light of the tasks carried out by all the other CEOs in municipalities in the same country. *Since the link between 'task' and 'demand' is mediated through this fundamental dependency among organizations within a country, we interpret the link in institutional terms rather than purely technical contingency terms.*

Other Factors at the Level of Organizational Field: Self-definition and Density of the Field

In the final part of this chapter, we will describe the organizational fields of municipalities in each country by a number of factors that are interesting in an institutional light.

First, we will consider the density or connectedness of the field: how frequent is the interaction between the elements in the field as well as between each element and a central organization of elements? This is a fundamental question within institutional theory. The cohesion of the field helps constitute the field as such (DiMaggio & Powell 1991, 65). We assume that a field with frequent interactions will allow new ideas to diffuse more quickly. We also know from neo-institutional theory that field-wide organizations play an important role in the diffusion of ideas which help structure and define the field (Powell & DiMaggio 1991). In the municipal world, such a role may be played by a national association of municipalities.

From survey data, we know how frequently CEOs in each country interact with officials from the national association of local authorities. This is a rough measure; it does not inform us about the nature of the interaction nor its salience. Neither do we know what role the association of local authorities plays in each country.

Sweden scores high on both the role of the change agent and the frequency of interaction with the national association of municipalites. However, a general pattern among the countries is not clear, and Finland is again a very deviant case.

Consider next what is here called the 'self-definition of the field'. We are interested in whether CEOs think of their own sector as uniquely 'public' or whether they have something to share with managers in the private sector. Apart from the case of Finland, the data lead to the following hypothesis: If municipal CEOs define their own sector as uniquely 'public', this inhibits the idea of the CEO as a change agent from becoming too established in the field. Or stated in more positive terms: a municipal self-definition that emphasizes perceived similarity (Meyer 1994, 103) between the public and private sectors seems to make the municipal field more susceptible to such ideas as 'the CEO as a change agent'. This is logical because the ideological roots of the management ideals in New Public Management emphasize the private sector as a model for the public sector, and attempt to reduce the peculiarly 'public' aspects of public management. We should be careful here not to over-

Table 2.6: Change agent items in job postings compared to characteristics of organizational fields by country; ( ) = rank order.

Country	Denmark	Finland	Norway	The Netherlands	France	Sweden	UK
N*	35	25	40	24	59	32	19
Change Agent Mean Score	21 (2)	6 (7)	12 (5)	15 (3)	7 (6)	36 (1)	13 (4)
Density of the Field: frequency of communication with officials from nat'l. assoc. of local authorities	18 (4)	23 (1-2)	21 (3)	9 (6)	MIS	23 (1-2)	16 (5)
Self-definition: How useful are private managers in helping CEOs develop their own skills?	49 (2)	51 (1)	MIS	47 (4)	30 (6)	48 (3)	43 (5)
Penetration of Field by Travellers percentage of ads where consultant is used	63 (1)	0 (7)	5 (6)	54 (2)	19 (5)	47 (3)	26 (4)

* N: taken from job posting analysis. N in survey is higher.

specify a uni-directional link between the self-definition of the field and the adoption of the idea of the CEO as a change agent. It is quite likely that the adoption of particular management ideals over time also influences the dominant self-understanding in the field.

Our final variable is the use of 'travelling agents' in the various organizational fields, in practice this means consultants. Consultants are known to be 'merchants of meaning' (Czarniawska 1990) who help spread decontextualized ideals of management and organization in organizational fields, often without respect for the institutional specificities of organizations within the field (Røvik 1992).

The percentage of ads in which consultants are mentioned (as co-producers of the ad and/or as consultants in the selection and hiring process) correlates well with the occurrence of change agent items in the job postings. Denmark, Sweden, and the

Table 2.7: Correlation between various change agent items in the ads and the use of consultants; N = 234 (seven countries).

Change agent item	Correlated to consultant used in the ad (chi² test, p<= 0.1; * p <= 0.01)
To formulate goals	no
To formulate visions	yes
To change/to reform	yes*
Develop, e.g., develop service	yes*
Develop trade and commerce in the municipality	yes*
At least one of the above items	yes*

Netherlands are in the top group on both of these variables, the UK in the middle, and Norway, France and Finland at the bottom. In this analysis, Finland is no longer a deviant case.

What do consultants do with respect to diffusion of the idea of the CEO as a change agent?

Table 2.7 shows a pancultural analysis of the relation between various change agent items and the participation of a consultant company in the job posting.

Apparently, consultants play an important role in the promotion of the idea of the CEO as a change agent. Most of the change agent items occur significantly more often when a consultant participates in the job posting. This is due partly to country effects, but what is also found in an analysis within countries (not shown). One might hypothesize that the correlation between ideals of change and the use of consultants is due only to organizational size. Large organizations are more likely to engage consultants than smaller ones. This is confirmed by data. The size of the municipality and the use of consultants are positively and significantly correlated in Denmark, France, and the Netherlands, as well as in a pancultural analysis (not shown).

Table 2.8 reveals the interaction patterns between the involved variables. In order to avoid too small N's in each analysis, the analysis is only run on 'at least one change agent item'.

The table reveals quite clearly that although the use of consultants is related to organizational size, they play an independent role in the diffusion of the idea of the CEO as a change agent. Apart from its influence on the use of consultants, size itself does not play a significant role in the overall occurrence of change agent items.

The presence of consultants coincides with the presence of change agent items in the job postings. It is too early, of course, to conclude that consultants bring the idea of change as a part of management to the municipality. It is possible that municipalities preferring change also have a preference for consultants. Nevertheless, the above analysis suggests a significant pattern in theoretical as well as statistical terms.

Table 2.8: Correlation between size, consultants and change agent items in the job postings; (cross-tabulation with chi² test, P < 0.1; * = P < 0.01) N=212 (six countries).

	Size and at least one change agent item	Consultants and at least one change agent item	Size and at least one change agent item controlling for consultants	Consultants and at least one change agent item controlling for size
All 6 Countries (N=212)	yes	yes*	consultants involved: no N = 61 consultants not involved: no N = 151	>10,000: yes* N = 114 <10,000: yes N = 98

Conclusion

This example has abundantly illustrated the almost classical phenomenon in comparative analysis that each difference in dependent variables is often over-determined by differences in several potential independent variables. The conclusion is written with this general caveat in mind.

In the countries analyzed in this chapter, job postings have expanded over a twenty-year period from brief formal announcements to elaborate discourses related to management, organization, and marketing.

The actual tasks of the individual jobs do not help us very much in explaining why job postings mention certain items such as those concerning the CEO as a change agent. In a few instances there are even negative correlations between the priority given to certain tasks by the CEOs themselves in their daily life and the job posting items mentioning the corresponding tasks. Job postings may therefore be better understood as socially defined wishes rather than as technical pieces of communication revealing distinctive information about a particular job.

Organizational size does not help us much in explaining the occurrence of change agent themes in job postings for municipal CEOs, at least only in country specific ways (in Norway, for example, it is the small municipalities which ask for change agents).

When we move to the ecological analysis (country-by-country comparison), we do not cancel out tasks and organizational size from our hypotheses about what influences the items in the job postings. When the classical bureaucratic role is important, and when the country has small municipalities, the idea of a change agent is less dominant among CEO job postings. In other words, when one municipality defines the content of its job postings, the typical size of other municipalities and the typical tasks of CEOs in other municipalities in the country seem to make a difference. The municipalities within a country are not independent.

This motivates our interest in factors at the level of organizational field. Correlated to the idea of the CEO as a change agent is also the self-definition of the field, i.e. the perceived specificity of public sector management as measured by the perceived relevance of managers in the private sector as role models. Somewhat more loosely connected to the job postings are the frequency of interactions between municipal CEOs and the national association of local authorities.

Finally, we have examined the role of consultants. Over and above their more frequent appearance in large municipalities, they are themselves a contributing factor to the diffusion of the idea of the CEO as a change agent. Most of the change agent items are more strongly correlated to the presence of consultants than any of the other explanatory factors.

As a final note, let us return to the concept of 'organizationability.' Some degree of 'organizationability' is needed for the CEO to be mentioned as a change agent in the job postings. Organizationability can be reduced if a particular organizational structure is institutionalized and perhaps centrally determined in a country. Organizationability tends to be reduced in a country where the municipalities are small for historical, political and institutional reasons. It may also be reduced if the CEO is closely tied up to such traditional bureaucratic tasks, such as ensuring that rules and regulations are followed.

On the other hand, in countries where a certain level of organizationability has been reached, factors in the organizational field help promote such a management ideal as the CEO as a change agent. Among these factors are the self-definition of the field (the degree to which the organizations in the field perceive themselves as unique versus able to learn from private managers) and the use of consultants. Consultants can then 'play' with the theme of organizationability, promoting a role for CEOs as change agents.

In this light, organizational size and managerial tasks should be understood within a perspective on organizational fields as social constructions rather than within a classical contingency perspective. What we have shown is that within these fields, various broad ideas such as the idea of the CEO as a change agent have systematically different chances of survival.

In other words, the broad changes which have recently affected local administrative systems have also affected the requirements made on the qualifications of CEOs. However, the definition of 'requirements' on the job is far from a purely technical one. It is mediated and moulded at the level of organizational fields and through idea brokers – better known as consultants.

All in all, changes in structures and tasks in local government management are in no way automatically and technically transformed into requirements for applicants to managerial positions. The process involves social, institutional and organizational definitions and translations rather than mathematical formulae.

Chapter 3

Background and Recruitment Characteristics of European CEOs

BY IRENE DELGADO, LOURDES LÓPEZ NIETO AND ELISEO LÓPEZ

Introduction

Most of the countries in Northern Europe have gone from a system with small municipalities to a system of relatively few but large municipalities. In some cases, they have at the same time evolved from a system with only elected laymen to a system with elected politicians assisted by numerous pure administrators. Hand in hand with the amalgamation reforms, more and more tasks have been delegated to the municipal level, especially those services which are central to the welfare state. In the countries of Southern Europe with a Napoleonic tradition (favouring centralization and hierarchy in public administration), the amalgamation reforms did not take place, as was the case in Spain, Italy or France. In these countries, the number of municipalities remains high. The heterogeneity of the municipalities should also be pointed out. Differences in geographical position, population size and economic aspects make it difficult to make any generalizations.

In Spain, for instance, the distribution of competences between actors and levels of government is still very complex and a continual topic of debate. In the Northern European countries, many tasks are performed by the municipalities. The variation of solutions between different municipalities is quite obvious: in Sweden, for example, municipalities can choose to have a CEO or can choose not to have one.

The processes of unification and reduction of the number of municipalities in the Northern European countries have taken place together with reform processes of their local government. The 1970s saw a rationalization of the local government followed by a modernization of the local administration, all of which transformed the frameworks of the municipality. These changes have not only affected the role of the CEO but also the recruitment and selection processes. The recent legal reforms of local government which have taken place in Southern European countries, have not affected local administration in the same way as in the Northern countries. The role of the CEO in Southern Europe is still more 'classical'. In Spain and in Italy, the CEO maintains the legal control of financial acts and administrative features of the municipalities. In Northern European countries, the trend is towards a CEO who is both an administrative leader and the link between the political and administrative levels of the municipalities. In this chapter, we shall focus on the main differences between Northern and Southern Europe.

The aim of this chapter is to elucidate the most relevant characteristics about recruitment and background of the European CEOs, taking into account the diversity of the municipalities in these countries. We shall examine such factors as gender, age, and educational background.

Social Characteristics

Gender

The CEO job attracts mostly men, but the overall distribution shows some difference between the north and the south of Europe. Female representation varies substantially across countries (fig. 3.1). In Denmark, just 15 years ago all 275 Danish CEOs were men, today 7 per cent are women; and among those hired within the last five years, the percentage is 12. In Southern Europe this change is slower, but the female proportion is higher. In Italy, Portugal, and Spain, 20 to 30 per cent of the CEOs are women. In France and in Belgium as well, 13 per cent of all municipal secretaries are women. These figures are the result of a trend of increasing feminization as it has occurred in other aspects of public life: since the mid-1960s, women have moved gradually towards increased representation in many European countries, although their proportion remains far from parity (Lowenduski 1986; Lowenduski & Norris 1993). Indeed, in Belgium, while all CEOs who have been longer than 30 years in service are men, this proportion is reduced to 76% males for those CEOs having less than 5 years of service.

A high proportion of women is common in countries where CEOs are recruited through a national competition, as is the case in Southern Europe (Magnier 1997). In those countries, women tend to prefer public employment over private jobs and are far from the entrepreneur role that prevails in Northern Europe. The model of public employment for CEOs in Southern Europe may be more compatible with the domestic tasks associated with a conventional female gender role.

In Denmark, more than two-thirds of those working in local administration are women, and they especially dominate the sectors linked to welfare (Albæk et al. 1996). Women tend to be underrepresented in the technical, financial and management sectors, and these are the areas where the municipal CEO is located.

Age

Most CEOs start their career rather young. Their average age at the time of the survey was 49 years, but again there are differences between the North and the South of Europe (fig. 3.2). A considerable number of CEOs belong to the younger generation, with the highest proportion in Spain, Italy, Belgium and France. The oldest CEOs are

Figure 3.1: Gender issues: female proportion of CEOs by country.

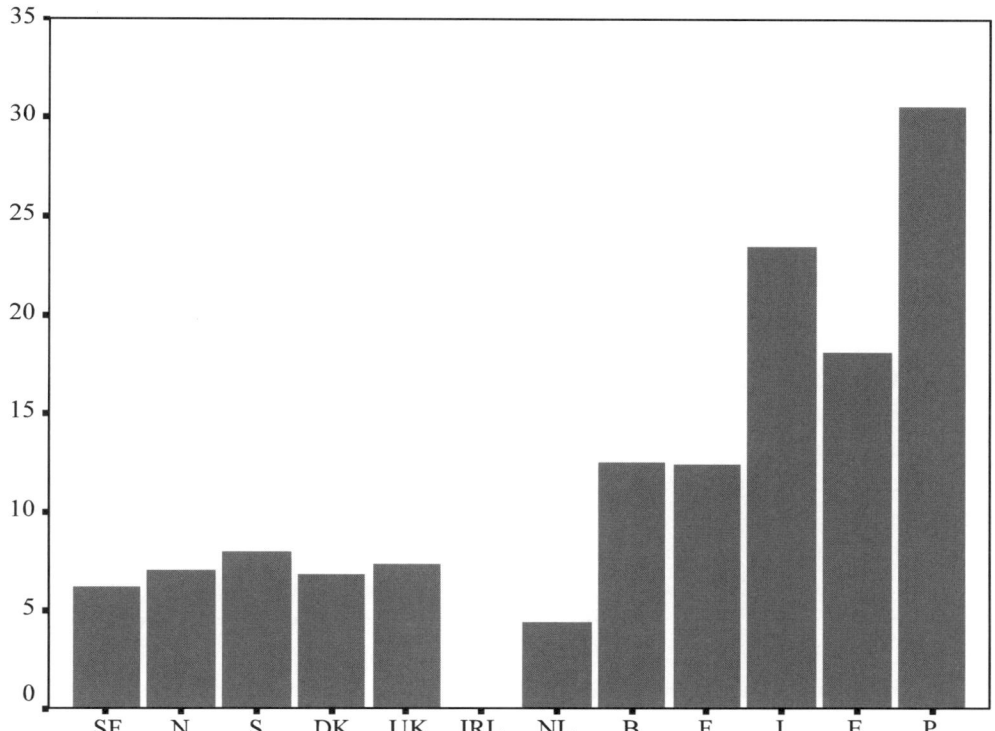

found in Ireland, Finland and the UK. The average age of the Spanish CEOs is 43 years, 75 per cent are 48 or younger and due to the training requirements of this profession first started performing their functions after age 25. In Italy, the mean age of CEOs is 48; in Belgium and France 46, and in Portugal 47 years.

Between 1989 and 1997, the total number of CEO posts in Spain has increased by 47%. This explains why Spanish CEOs are the youngest in the sample.

The age profile of CEOs could be significant if, as Inglehart suggests, the younger generation brought with them to public life a distinctive set of values and priorities (Inglehart 1977; 1991; Abramson & Inglehart 1995).

Education
Among the present European CEOs, a high percentage (61,3%) have academic degrees (table 3.1). The most common university degrees are in law, followed by political science and economics. In addition a few have non-social science educations, such as technical fields, natural sciences and humanities/history.

Figure 3.2: Average ages of European CEOs.

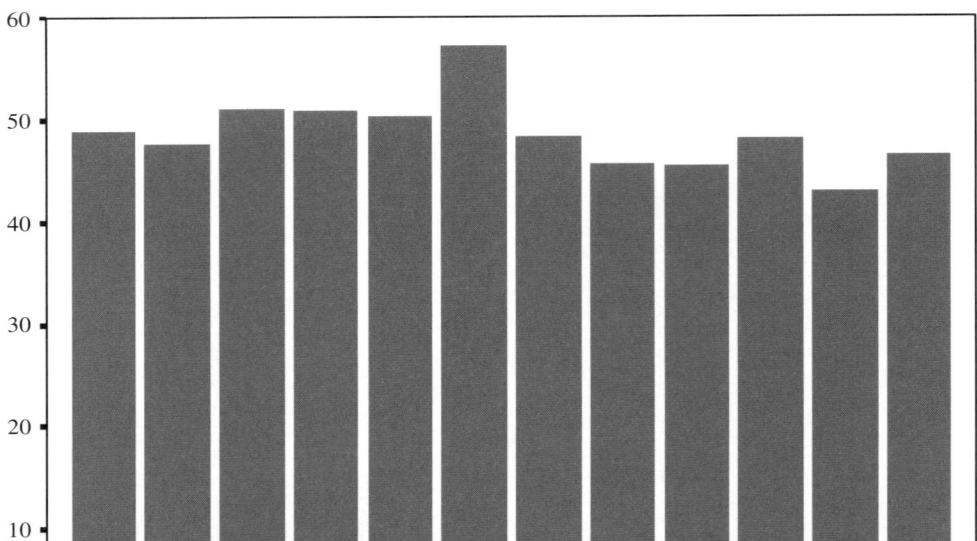

Table 3.1: Educational background of CEOs in eight countries *.

University degree	Country									45 years or younger
	N	S	DK	UK	IRL	B	E	P	All	
Law	213	26	16.5	274	5	17	559	298	26	41
Economics	11.8	28.1	11.7	10	193	8.4	1.9	15.6	13	13
Political Science	11.6	47.1	7.9	108	16.7	19.5	33	4.4	15	16
Technical degree	5.7	3.6	0.5	10.0	9.7	1.4	0.4	-	4	1
Humanity	4.4	3.7	1	14.3	2.9	4.3	5.7	2.2	4	5
Other	-	24.8	6.4	15.3	19.8	10.3	3.1	5	12	9
Any university degree	48.7	95	43.6	74.6	51.2	51.3	81.8	44.1	61	74
Any university degree among 45 years old or younger	47.2	100	70.3	85.6	-	68.8	84.4	80	74	-
N	324	223	200	284	21	352	188	104	1696	547

* The table includes 8 countries in which fairly comparable categorizations of educational background were carried out in the U.Di.T.E. survey.

The role of the CEO as a legal controller is reflected in the high proportion of Spanish CEOs with legal degrees. The same is true for Italy (not displayed in table 3.1), where two-thirds of the CEOs have a degree in law (Magnier 1997).

In some cases, such as Belgium, the educational background of the CEO is often supplemented by complementary administrative education, e.g., courses organized by the provinces or by the national association of municipal CEOs. Yet in Belgium, there remain impressive differences in educational background among the regions. Large municipalities nevertheless tend to have CEOs with university degrees, which is partly due to recruitment regulations (Plees & Laurent 1998, 177-8).

In Denmark, local authorities have traditionally dealt with the training of their own administrative staff, including their chief officers. Since the early 1930s, a whole training system has gradually been established for local authority administrative staff consisting of courses at the college of local government and the Danish school of administration, but these are not degree courses (Albæk *et al.* 1996). However, this type of education of CEOs will not be typical in the future.

The bottom row includes only CEOs aged 45 years or younger. Although the data set itself is static, a comparison of young CEOs to all is likely to be indicative of changes in the composition of the corps of CEOs in each country. The proportion holding university degrees seems to increase over time. This tendency is very clear in Denmark, Belgium, and Portugal. An academic upgrading seems to be the order of the day in most countries, Norway excepted. This finding conforms to Putnam (1976) who found that one of the most striking long-term trends in public life is the gradual increase in the proportion of university-educated managers. Among the young CEOs (45 years or less) in all eight countries, 74.8% hold university degrees (compared to 61.3% of all CEOs regardless of age).

The two columns to the right in table 3.1. show the types of university degrees held by all CEOs and by CEOs who are 45 or younger, respectively. Again the data set is static, but the younger CEOs signify the likely future more than does the whole corps of CEOs. The young CEOs distinguish themselves by the much higher proportion holding a law degree.

Conclusion

To summarize, we see rather drastic changes in the background of European CEOs. To an increasing extent, the job has been taken over by persons with academic degrees. These changes started to take place in the 1970s, continued in the early 1980s and accelerated from the mid- or late 1980s. In short, they reflect or they are in accordance with the dramatic changes in the environment of administrative leaders which has taken place within the last few years and which definitely requires other qualifications than was the case a decade or two ago.

In contrast with the North European countries, we have seen in the South a traditional model of local administrative leaders. More hesitation with administrative reforms and the stability of this scenario affect the development of the CEOs' basic task. In Northern Europe, the changes in the environment have radically affected the CEOs. They have assumed the role of managers in a complex arena, in which the local government carries out the main functions of the welfare state, such as education or health care. These areas require specialized knowledge in public management in order to satisfy the growing demands of the citizens. This implies that the CEO has a qualified professional profile. Their careers become rather more similar to a manager of a private company than to an official public servant. A manager is hired for a specific length of time in order to achieve some specific objectives. These are measured not only in money but also in social satisfaction and political convenience. The CEO entrepreneur leaves the municipality after completion of the contract – like the manager of a private company. They look for another municipality. This is the new model of employment, although it is far from implemented everywhere.

In contrast, the South European countries continue to preserve the CEO as the classical financial and legal controller, but the evolution has taken a different direction. Typically, there has been an increase in qualifications as a requirement to enter the career, which is still a stable and secure position.

In fact, all of the main characteristics we have pointed to are in accordance with the two basic types of CEOs, related to the way the level of modernization of the local government in their respective countries has developed. Yet there are some common features, such as *the higher educational degrees of CEOs, but the causes that produce them are different.* There continues to be a real difference between the North and the South of Europe.

CHAPTER 4

Beyond the City Hall: Municipal Administrative Leadership and Local Community

BY ANNICK MAGNIER

Introduction

How 'local' are local CEOs? What are their relations with the citizenry? What kind of bonds tie them to their local communities? A discussion of the various dimensions of CEOs' 'localism' relates to the question of the possible persistence of local public action and local bureaucracy in the context of multi-level governance.

We shall use the data on the geographical origins of the CEOs, their professional socialization and their attitude towards the local community as well as interpretations of these same data offered in the first comparative report on the research (Klausen & Magnier 1998). The analysis of the local dimension of professional socialization will be based on a discussion of the career paths of the CEOs.

Restructuring Local Government, CEOs and Communities

The role of CEOs across countries varies considerably. The common definition of the CEO as the 'formal leader of the municipal administration' has very different meanings. Basic functions are common to all the national cases (notary functions of the acts of the municipality, responsibility of the minutes of the meetings of the council and the executive boards, legal advisory functions for the political sphere; and, except in Portugal and in the Council-Mayor systems, coordination of the administrative department activities). The main differences concern: (1) the possible transformation of responsibility in the *a priori* control of the legality of acts originating in the municipality (this function, while central in the definition of the role in the Napoleonic model, was progressively reduced in the countries of the Franco-group, it is highly significant also in other areas, even if not similarly codified); (2) the possible transformation of coordinating activities in true administrative leadership (i.e. covering such areas as selection, training and management of human resources, and the overall responsibility for administrative efficiency and for the quality of results towards politicians or towards the administrative hierarchy).

The differences are still important, but the diachronic picture (as offered in Klausen & Magnier 1998) is quite clear: it shows the growing emphasis on the capacity of local CEOs as *administrative leaders*.

Further uniform trends emerge from the diachronic analysis of the structures offered in the first U.Di.T.E. report (Klausen & Magnier 1998). The trend towards privatization and contracting-out while strongly represented in Anglo-Saxon literature (Walsh 1995; Stewart & Stoker 1995), is not confined to this area.[1] In countries where local government plays an extensive role in the provision of services in the welfare state, such as in Northern Europe, but also to some extent in the countries of Southern Europe, 'externalization' transforms the municipalities from service providers to regulatory agencies. This is often followed by a multiplication of the entities expressing political demands. In addition, a declining influence of the large parties has created a scenario of fragmented and weaker majorities.

The fragmentation of the majorities and weakening of the political sphere, together with the transformation of the functions of the municipalities, should suggest a re-centralization of 'executive' competence of appointed public managers. CEOs in most countries speak of a growing delegation of tasks from politicians to bureaucrats, particularly in Sweden, Denmark, the Netherlands and Australia.

The Slow Convergence of Career Patterns: the Enlarged World of Local Authorities as the Main Socialization Agency

Does today's professional socialization of our CEOs prepare them to form close relations with their local communities? The U.Di.T.E. survey offers two sets of information on the current career schemes: (1) the position of the CEOs' first job, which is a strategic stage in their *work history* and extremely influential in their socialization to work; and (2) their most recent job prior to their current position. These data, while not sufficient to show precise *career lines* (Hughes 1951; Spilerman 1977; Spenner-Orro-Call 1982), nevertheless help us discern the main features of differentiated career patterns.

To assess the current congruence of the CEOs' career with the traditional images offered in the comparative tradition of local political-administrative systems, we shall distinguish between *bureaucratic* careers, institutionally rigidly defined in their design and tempo, and *innovative* careers, which are more diversified and personalized, and constructed by the individuals according to their ambitions and capacities in a less 'contrived' institutional framework (Hughes 1951). Rigidly *bureaucratic* is the *separate career* of the *secrétaire municipal,* a controller of local authorities whose mobility is narrowly controlled by central government, in the countries of the so-called Franco-group. Also *bureaucratic* was the very different internal *bottom-up*

---

[1] A unique exception: in Portugal, a vast majority of the CEOs interviewed declare that during the last decade there has not been privatization or contracting out in their municipality.

career of municipal clerks who rose to the summit position of CEO, a typical trajectory in certain Anglo-Saxon countries.

Using the first and the previous position of CEOs as our reference points, we shall distinguish five career patterns: (1) a *mixed innovative career* includes at least one job in the private sector (including unions and third sector); (2) an *innovative public career* includes only positions in public administration or public services but at least one experience outside the world of municipalities (associations of local authorities are not included in world of municipalities); (3) a *separate career* includes only CEO positions; (4) a *bottom-up career* is located exclusively in municipalities and includes a promotion to the position of CEO from another position in the same municipality; and (5) an *innovative local career* if the jobs have been located exclusively within municipalities but include an appointment in another municipality. Each career path can be categorized as only one of the above patterns. Although these are imperfect analytical instruments, they allow for a synthetic indicative cross-national comparison.[2]

When we examine data describing the first job of the CEOs (table 4.1), conventional images begin to fade. Except in Spain (where a majority of CEOs were socialized to work precisely as CEO), in all the countries considered, the first working experiences of Western CEOs mainly took place in the enlarged municipal sphere; or for a significant minority, in the private sector. Municipal administration is a typical socialization agency in Finland (for 60% of the Finnish CEOs), but also in Sweden, the Netherlands, Denmark, Ireland and France. In all these countries, the proportion of CEOs who began to work in a City Hall in a position different from that of CEO exceeds 40%. The private sector (very weakly represented in the Netherlands) is especially influential in the UK, Australia (where almost half the CEOs were socialized to the working world in private firms) and in Italy.[3] On the contrary, a career path through county and regional bodies tends to be very rare (reaching around 5% only in Australia, Norway and the Netherlands). This illustrates the persistent separateness of the world of municipalities among 'local' bodies in Western democracies. Not surprisingly, the presence of central government positions among entry-level jobs is more significant in Sweden (more then 20%); in many countries they represent around 10% of the first working experiences. However, they are exceptionally rare in the UK, the Netherlands, Italy, Spain and Australia. The third sector has very little influence on CEOs' first work socialization.

From this quick overview, two main features appear: (1) a significant interaction

---

[2] The measure of 'bottom-up' careers is especially unsatisfactory, and the dimensions of the phenomenon are presumably emphasized: we do not know whether or not the first position of our CEOs was in the same municipality. The lack of data concerning the entrance jobs in the USA also limits the possibility of comparison.

[3] A unique exception: Portugal, in which the large majority of the interviewed CEOs declared that there has not been any privatization or contracting out in their municipality in the last decade.

Table 4.1: The present CEOs' first job after full-time education. %. (N = 3216).[4]

	CEO	Private sector	Municipal world*	County-regions**	Central administration***	Local Authorities' associations	Third sector	Unions	N
Finland	1.6	7.2	61.3	1.3	20.5	7.7	-	0.3	320
Norway	2.0	13.6	40.5	6.5	35.6	0.6	0.3	0.9	312
Sweden	-	9.0	44.4	3.8	40.6	1.8	-	0.4	210
Denmark	9.4	15.4	50.9	5.4	23.2	4,7	-	-	198
UK	-	47.3	31.1	3.3	18.3	-	-	-	281
Ireland	-	21.7	58.4	-	19.8	-	-	-	21
The Netherlands	2.6	5.4	67.8	4.0	18.7	1.5	-	-	384
Belgium	5.2	29.1	26.4	3.0	33.7	1.0	0.6	1.0	310
France	4.0	23.0	40.9	1.8	28.5	0.6	1.2	-	259
Italy	36.2	35.5	6.7	2.9	18.5	-	-	0.1	400
Spain	59.2	17.6	13.3	-	9.6	-	-	0.2	183
Portugal	-	24.1	36.5	-	39.4	-	-	-	98
Australia	1.3	47.6	38.1	6.6	6.5	-	-	-	240

*   Includes, except for the position of CEO, all municipal positions marked 20-27 in our international coding.
** All positions listed in regional and county bodies (codes 30-38).
*** Includes all other positions in public bodies and services, but also in QUANGOs (codes 40-70).

with the whole world of 'public service' and sometimes with the private sector; (2) a limited interaction with other levels of decentralized non-municipal government.

Table 4.2 shows the various career patterns. Far from adapting to *bureaucratic,* rigidly ordered career ladders, CEOs often seem to have carved out their own career path according to their capacities and desires, principally in local government positions, but also in other public and third sector positions, sometimes jumping from private sector to public sector positions. Using our basic typology, we observe (1) the

---

[4] The data on the USA are not available; the question (c8) was not included in the national questionnaire.

Beyond the City Hall

rarity of internal *bottom-up* careers (the number of which is probably overestimated), (2) the dominant presence of *innovative* public and local careers, but also (3) a more than marginal mix between public and private experiences. Our data show that the 'Napoleonic' model, according to which central authorities lay out fixed bureaucratic, 'separate' career schemes for municipal CEOs, is no longer dominant on the scene in the 'Franco-group' countries, although frequent in Italy and Spain.

Some of the career patterns are typical of specific countries. Yet with Spain as an exception, the innovative career path is dominant everywhere. Most career patterns are centered on the public sector (except in Australia and in the UK). The local level strongly dominates, except in Norway, Sweden, and Belgium).

Table 4.2: Career patterns. %. (N=3055).

	Bottom-up	Separate	Innovative local	Innovative public	Mixed	N
Finland	11.0	2.2	43.5	32.0	11.3	319
Norway	10.1	4.2	20.3	45.0	20.3	303
Sweden	16.5	-	20.1	52.3	11.0	208
Denmark	20.8	0.5	27.7	35.4	15.6	195
UK	11.9	-	18.0	23.3	46.8	266
Ireland	23.9	-	29.5	24.9	21.7	21
The Netherlands	19.9	0.5	39.6	34.1	5.9	382
Belgium	16.1	5.0	7.2	37.5	34.2	286
France	13.6	5.0	25.3	32.2	23.9	252
Italy	0.9	44.4	3.8	19.6	31.2	326
Spain	2.3	50.9	14.9	11.4	20.5	172
Portugal	22.4	-	10.0	40.6	27.1	90
Australia	5.4	0.8	31.7	14.3	47.8	235

Increased predominance of academic education contributes further to the decline of the *bottom-up* career. We saw (in Chapter 3 as well as in Klausen & Magnier 1998) that a university degree is now practically a prerequisite for access to the position as CEO in all the Western local governments. In only two countries, Finland and Denmark, do non-academics still hold many CEO positions.

While unconventional career patterns are thus revealed, the previous chapter shows that the re-definitions of the selection and training of local CEOs are matched only by incremental changes, not by institutional activities in favour of extensive reforms concerning formation, selection and training. The patterns of selection, more than any other feature, are still the intricate expressions of the history of the role. Only the Napoleonic model of career, based on national selection through written examinations and authoritarian appointment[5] to a specific position, has been

---

5   Even if agreed through informal contacts between politicians.

systematically reformed: today we find it only in Portugal, though extremely limited by the mayor's power to demand the dismissal of the CEO, and in Spain, where it is corrected by the intense use of interim nominations by the mayor out of the national rolls. In Ireland, rigid control on the recruitment is still exerted by the Central Authorities through the examination procedure. The CEO is chosen by the mayor and by the executive board in France, Sweden, Israel, and sometimes in the United States;[6] and by the Council in Belgium, the Netherlands, the UK, Finland, Denmark, and often in the United States. The mayor's influence on the nomination (significant nowadays in all countries abandoning the Napoleonic career model) seems generally to increase. However, while CEOs are often locally chosen, the decentralization of their selection goes hand in hand with a substantial 'de-localization' of their work history. Careers center mainly on local government, but the CEOs are often geographically mobile: through their jobs, CEOs are socialized into a municipal world rather than to a specific community.

Quite often, the CEOs studied have no roots in the region where they now live.[7] Only in Norway, Italy, Spain, the United States and Australia, did more than half the CEOs spend part of their childhood in the region where they presently work (80% in Australia). Seventy-three per cent of the CEOs live within the boundaries of their employing authority (less in the UK, in Spain and overall in Italy). However, they do not participate very actively in the life of local associations. There are exceptions in Ireland, where CEOs on average belong to five local associations, in Australia (4.1), and in Finland (4), while CEOs are veritable 'foreigners' in the local associational life in Norway (2), the UK (1.5), Italy (0.4) and Spain (0.7).

Conclusion

These few data on CEOs' local roots confirm the dominant image of local CEOs as formed by their career patterns. Local CEOs are a status group whose professionalization is based on specific resources such as an academic background (relatively often in law) and a know-how acquired in many loci within the world of public bodies and public services. CEOs are 'local' mainly in the sense that their work histories tie them to the world of local government, but they have few roots in the local community. CEOs are nearer to the model of the medieval *podestà* than to the *primus inter pares* of a street level bureaucracy. *Through their jobs, CEOs are socialized into a municipal world not to a specific community.*

---

[6] From 1997 in Italy, too, the CEO is chosen by the mayor; at the moment of our survey, he/she was still designated by the Central Government following ambiguous procedures of professional and political consultation.

[7] Some discrepancies in the figures of this table and the successive ones are associated with differences in the number of respondents to the two questions.

CHAPTER 5

Values of Local Government CEOs in Job Motivation: How Do CEOs See the Ideal Job?

BY MIKAEL SØNDERGAARD

Introduction

City managers run our cities, but nobody knows why they are doing it, or what they are getting out of it.[1] Motivation structures, in terms of attitudes and values, can provide us with an insight into questions about why these people seek the job of managing our cities.

This chapter takes a closer look at the motives of those seeking the job as chiefs of the civil service of local government. Amongst the many factors involved in being attracted to and choosing to work in local public life, motivation will be singled out as the explanatory factor. Values of CEOs related to practices and styles of leadership will be dealt with elsewhere in the U.Di.T.E. book series.

More precisely, the ideas of the ideal job, assumed to be close to the job held as CEO, will be analyzed as motivational factors. A number of researchers have found a link between job motivation and choice of job (Hofstede 1989, 1984; Ronen 1986; Posner & Munson 1979; Terpstra 1980; Kanungo & Wright 1983).

Someone interested in management positions in organizations with a fast career track and emphasis on results and material benefits is likely to seek employment in a different kind of organization than those persons attracted to management positions in organizations with secure employment and emphasis on social relations and public goods. Our interest in matching personal goals with type of work organization follows earlier research tracks, one of which was founded by Argyris in the 1950s (Argyris 1954; 1957).

Values regarding work-life are likely to reflect more fundamental attitudes towards key issues of how to organize the public work situation, e.g.,

---

[1] An initial version of this paper was presented at the 25th ECPR Joint Workshops in Bern 1997, in the session on 'Local Elites in a Comparative Perspective.'

1) who is deciding how much and how?
2) to what extent should work processes be standardized by rules?
3) how are subordinates motivated to work more efficiently and with more satisfaction?

The influence of national culture and organizational culture on management ideas has been one of the main topics of the organizational science literature of the 1980s. One tradition of demonstrating the influence of national culture on work values and situations has been to compare groups of people who are similar in several aspects presumed to affecting work values: type of organization, work function, age, and level of education. In this methodological tradition, equally unrepresentative national groups, say French and Danish nurses or medical doctors, are sampled for comparison rather than representative samples of national populations. Participants in the U.Di.T.E. leadership study constitute well-matched samples in many respects, except nationality. The job context of the participants varies greatly depending on difference in task and in organizational size. This difference is a within country difference and is most likely to exist in any of the countries of the study. Given the sample construction, the task and size variance should not disturb the between-country comparisons.

The idea thus emerged to carry out a comprehensive replication of a classic study of work values of IBM employees of the late 1960s and early 1970s. From the IBM study, Dutch professor Geert Hofstede proposed a workable and rather precise framework of four dimensions to describe differences in values related to the work situation.

In 1980, Hofstede published *Culture's Consequences*. The analysis of survey answers by 130,000 IBM employees in 40 countries, the largest organizational study so far, resulted in four dimensions to describe how different countries have dealt with universal issues such as

1) inequality of power, i.e. power distance,
2) unpredictable situations with which people have to deal, given the future is unknown, i.e. uncertainty avoidance, and
3) the ways in which members of a society define themselves and
4) their roles vis-á-vis others, i.e. individualism and masculinity.

Hofstede located his dimensions in terms of national cultures, not of personalities. These dimensions do not describe individuals. They describe differences in dominant patterns of socialization in nations.

The four dimensions of the framework are defined as:

1. Power distance measures differences in acceptance of unequal power distribution in a society.[2] Power distance is the extent to which the less powerful members of institutions and organizations within a society expect and accept that power is distributed unequally.
2. Individualism versus Collectivism.[3] At the pole of individualism, we find a society where members have learned to think for themselves. Everyone is expected to look after himself or herself and his/her immediate family only. The pole of collectivism pertains to societies in which people from birth are integrated into strong, cohesive groups which protect them in return for unquestioning loyalty throughout their life.
3. Masculinity versus Femininity.[4] Masculinity denotes a society in which social gender roles are clearly distinct. Men are supposed to be assertive, tough and focused on material success. Women are supposed to be more modest, tender and concerned with the quality of life. The opposite pole of this dimension is Femininity. Femininity stands for a society in which social gender roles overlap. Men and women are supposed to be modest, tender, and concerned with the quality of life.
4. Uncertainty Avoidance is the extent to which the members of institutions and organizations within a society feel threatened by uncertain, unknown, ambiguous, or unstructured situations and have created institutions and practices to avoid such situations.[5] The dimension measures a preference for structured over unstructured situations. Structured situations are those in which there are clear written as well as unwritten rules as to how one should behave.

---

[2] The 'Power Distance' dimension is based on the following questions: 'Please think of an ideal job – disregarding your present job. In choosing an ideal job, how important would it be for you to:' – specifically the items: 'Have a good working relationship with your direct superiors?' and 'Be consulted by your direct superior in her/his decisions?'; 'In your experience, how frequently are subordinates afraid to express disagreement with their superiors?'. And, finally, 'To what extent do you agree or disagree with each of the following statements?' item: 'An organization structure in which certain subordinates have two bosses should be avoided at all cost'.

[3] The 'Individualism' dimension is based on the following questions: 'Please think of an ideal job – disregarding your present job. In choosing an ideal job, how important would it be for you to:' – specifically the items: 'Have sufficient time for your personal or family life?'; 'Have good physical working conditions?'; 'Have security of employment?' and, finally, 'Have an element of variety and adventure in the job?'.

[4] The 'Masculinity' dimension is based on the following questions: 'Please think of an ideal job – disregarding your present job. In choosing an ideal job, how important would it be to you to:' – specifically the items: 'Work with people who cooperate well with one another?' and 'Have an opportunity for advancement to higher level jobs?' and 'To what extent do you agree or disagree with each of the following statements?' items: 'Most people can be trusted' and 'When people have failed in life it is often their own fault'.

[5] The 'Uncertainty Avoidance' dimension is based on the following questions: 'How often do you feel nervous or tense at work?' and 'To what extent do you agree or disagree with each of the following statements?' items: 'One can be a good manager without having precise answers to most questions that subordinates may raise about their work'; 'Competition between employees usually does more harm than good' and, finally, 'The rules of an organization should not be broken – not even when the employee thinks it is in the best interest of the organization'.

Hofstede's fifth dimension, long-term vs short-term orientation, has not been included in this study. The fifth dimension is appropriate in comparisons between Asian and Western countries.

It was decided to use a more recent and less IBM-specific version of the value survey module than the one used in the original study. Based on a number of replications in other types of organizations, Hofstede (1994c) made publicly available a value survey module of a more general nature, and this survey has been used with permission in the U.Di.T.E. study (1996).

Work Related Value Findings of the U.Di.T.E. Study

The findings of the Hofstede dimensions from the U.Di.T.E. study are listed in table 5.1.

Table 5.1: Country scores of cultural difference on four dimensions in three country groups.

Country	Power Distance	Individuality	Masculinity	Uncertainty Avoidance
Finland	27	88	-42	10
Norway	20	121	-38	-27
Sweden	25	112	-58	-8
Denmark	10	123	-34	-34
The UK	12	122	4	22
Ireland	21	108	12	-8
USA	19	115	11	29
Australia	22	120	-6	21
The Netherlands	30	97	-31	18
Belgium	31	94	-10	104
France	34	90	8	89
Italy	14	81	19	90
Spain	31	64	9	120
Portugal	35	89	20	73

Hofstede's concepts measure *differences* with respect to a number of values. The actual position, the score, is not as interesting as the relative positions of the country scores obtained by using the Hofstede formula. The scores of the 14 countries cluster in three groups: a Nordic group, an Anglo-Saxon group and a Southern European group. Some countries are 'stable', in that they are located in these groups on all four dimensions; others are less stable.

Indeed, a cluster analysis (K-means) using all four original dimensions to distinguish Western cultures (i.e. 'power distance', 'individualism', 'masculinity', 'uncertainty avoidance') produced three country clusters indicated in table 5.1. The Nordic country cluster consists of Finland, Norway, Sweden and Denmark. The Southern European country cluster includes Belgium, France, Italy, Spain and Portugal. The Anglo-Saxon country cluster contains the UK, Ireland, the USA, Australia and the Netherlands.

Data from the U.Di.T.E. leadership study show the expected differences between the Southern European countries: Portugal, France, Belgium and Spain score high on 'power distance' and 'uncertainty avoidance'. The Nordic countries, and a group of Anglo Saxon countries, i.e. the UK, Ireland, the United States and Australia, score, as usual, low on these dimensions. The Netherlands and Belgium belong to the group of Southern European countries on this dimension, whereas Italy belongs to the Nordic group. It is to be expected that the mid-European countries belong to different groupings, (Ronen 1986). It was unexpected that Italy did not fit into the Southern European pattern. A reexamination of the translation of the questionnaire did not find any sources of misunderstanding (personal correspondence with Hofstede 1997). A possible explanation is that Italian CEOs have a higher status and a more powerful position, since power distance is negatively related to degree of status, hierarchical position, and level of education (Hofstede 1994a, 28-31). This unexpected finding deserves further analysis.

The data analysis also shows that local government chiefs are all highly individualistic in their life orientations. Most individualistic are local government CEOs from the UK, as expected, and from Denmark. The less individualistically-oriented CEOs are found in Spain. By comparison, local government CEOs from Italy, Portugal, Finland and France are somewhat more individualistic.

Our analysis also indicates that all European local government CEOs score low on 'masculinity'. This indicates a very strong social interest and a commitment to the social welfare of the local community on the part of local government CEOs.

The care for the unfortunate, poor, sick, old, or unemployed is measured by the 'masculinity' dimension. As expected, CEOs from countries with a long tradition for welfare policy, such as Sweden, Finland, Denmark and the Netherlands, score lowest on masculinity. In comparison, CEOs from Portugal, Italy and France and Spain score high on masculinity.

Direct supervision, mutual adjustment and standardization represent three ways in which organizations coordinate their work. Direct supervision implies that one person is responsible for the work of others, issues direct instructions to them and monitors them directly. Mutual adjustment, on the other hand, means that those who perform a task control the work, using informal communication to adapt to each other along the way (Mintzberg 1983, 4).

Mutual adjustment and direct supervision are concepts associated with the use of hierarchical authority in the process of coordination of work. Mutual adjustment implies no usage of the hierarchy in the process of work coordination. Direct supervision, however, entails that the hierarchy is involved directly in the process of coordination. The vertical distance in an organizational hierarchy is associated with Hofstede's power distance. Coordination is achieved by standardization, e.g., by specifying the content of the work, the results of the work, or the kind of training required to perform the work (Mintzberg 1983, 5-6).

Figure 5.1: Coordination mechanisms. Position of 14 countries on power distance and uncertainty avoidance dimensions.

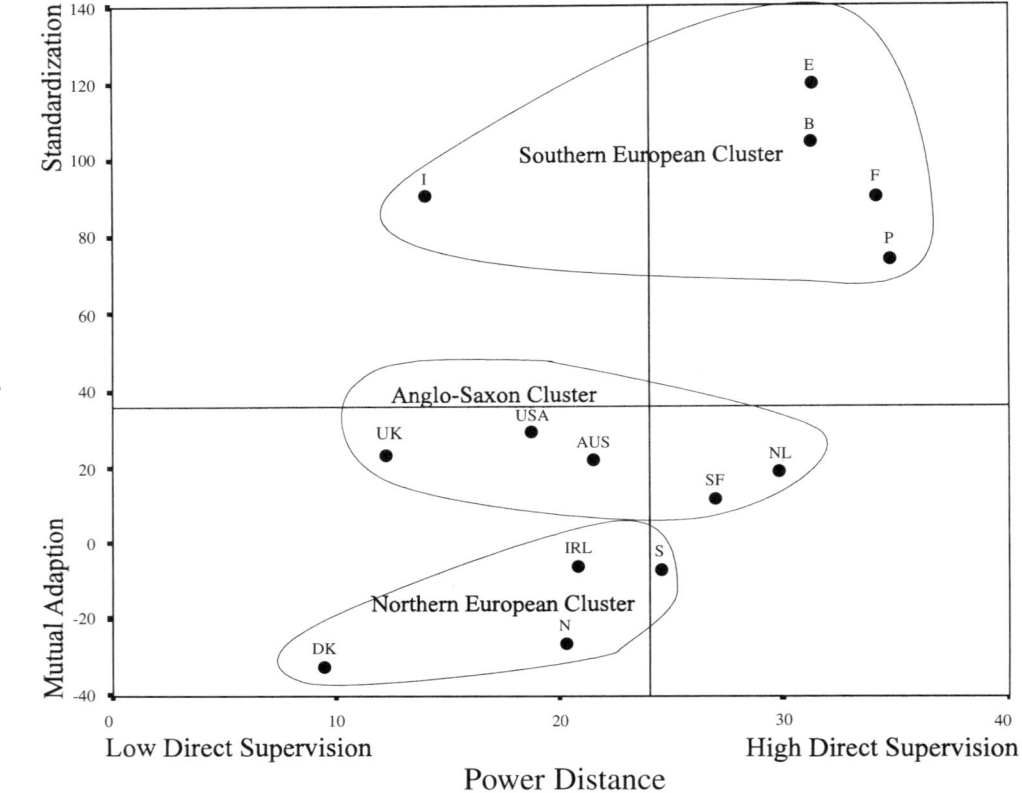

'Mutual adaptation' is a mechanism of coordination that fits with low degree uncertainty avoidance.[6] Standardization is a mechanism of coordination that fits with high degree uncertainty avoidance. Direct supervision is a mechanism of coordination that involves a degree of hierarchical activity. A high degree of direct supervision with high power distance. A low degree of direct supervision fits with low power distance.

A cluster analysis (K-means) produced three clusters: a Southern European cluster (Spain, Belgium, France, Portugal and Italy): a cluster of countries in Northern Europe (Denmark, Norway, Sweden and Ireland), and a cluster of most-

---

[6] 'Fit' is an illustrative point of reference. There is no empirical analysis of the correspondence between the preference of using rules, encouragement, and tasks and the Hofstede dimensions.

Figure 5.2: Motivation. Position of 14 countries on masculinity and uncertainty avoidance dimensions.

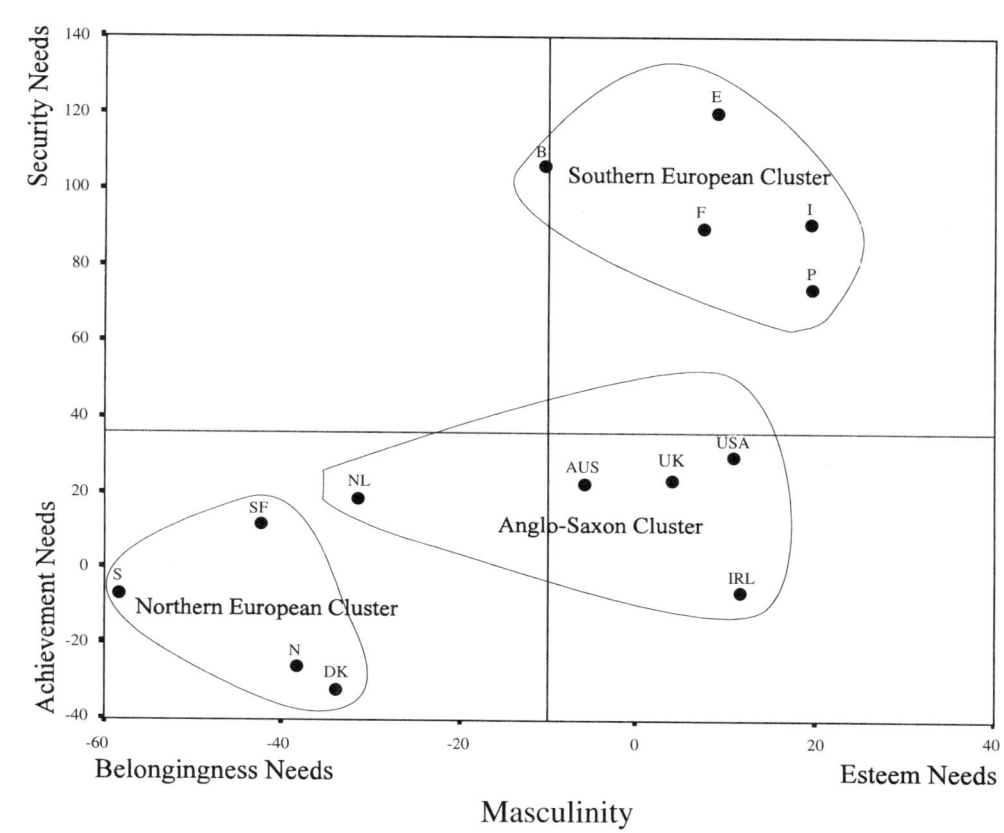

ly Anglo-Saxon Countries containing the UK, USA, Australia, Finland and the Netherlands.

Motivation, on the other hand, has been associated with satisfying a number of human needs, some of which can be connected to two of Hofstede's dimensions. The horizontal axis of figure 5.2 depicts belongingness needs versus esteem needs. These need categories fit with the masculinity dimension. The vertical axis shows achievement needs as opposed to security needs. These need categories fit with the uncertainty avoidance dimension. The cluster analysis (K-means) produced three clusters. The cluster of Southern European countries, i.e. Spain, Belgium, France, Portugal and Italy, indicates a preference for security and esteem needs. The cluster of Northern European countries, i.e. Denmark, Norway, Sweden and Finland, reflects needs for belongingness and achievement. The cluster of mostly Anglo-Saxon countries, i.e. the UK, USA, Australia, Ireland and the Netherlands, reflects esteem and achievement needs.

In the U.Di.T.E. study, we find three clusters of countries, Southern European,

Northern European and Anglo-Saxon, regardless of whether we cluster on the basis of all four dimensions of cultural difference or on pairs of dimensions. This pattern of differences between national groups of respondents seems non-random and stable. We have replicated the cultural regions identified by Ronen and Shenkar (1985), who reviewed eight studies where different measures for cultural values were used.

Our findings, furthermore, reconfirm a basic divide identified by Smith *et al.* (1996) who confirmed a major cultural divide between Southern and Northern Europe based on a study of a range of personal values and behavioral intentions of 10,000 managers and employees. Very similar country clusters were found in the variation of leadership prototypes across 22 European countries (Brodbeck *et al.* 2000).

Our U.Di.T.E. respondents fit the pattern of regional clusters of very *different* types of respondents surveyed on both value and behavioral intention issues. The profound nature of such groupings will also be illustrated by other issue areas analyzed in the U.Di.T.E. book series.

U.Di.T.E. Findings Compared with the Salzburg Seminar Alumni Study

The findings of the analysis of local government CEO values can also be compared to findings from a comparative study of *similar* national groups of people surveyed on *similar* value items. Hoppe compared work-related values among European alumni of the Salzburg seminar (Hoppe 1992). Participants to this seminar came from both the public and private sectors as well as from interest organizations. Although these participants are not as well matched as the local government CEOs, they constitute samples of elites from their respective countries. The participants in the Salzburg seminar consisted mainly of high ranking executives and officials in national organizations and institutions.

Comparing the results of the country elites with regional elites constituted by local government CEOs, we make a number of interesting observations. First, the relative difference between cultural clusters of country elites is in most cases the same as the difference between the regional elites.

Second, the country and local elites score very similarly on uncertainty avoidance. On the remaining dimensions we find a number of deviations. The scores of the regional elites have to be adjusted for age, education, and functions in order to be compared more precisely with the scores of the country elites. Further interpretation of the deviations will have to be carried out at a later date.

Work Motivation

Origins of Incentive Structures

Why do people work? Work is an important part of peoples' lives and associated with both pleasure and pain.

> 'Nature has placed mankind under the governance of two sovereign masters, pain and pleasure. It is from them alone to point out what we ought to do, as well as to determine what we shall do'(Bentham 1789, in Bakka & Fivelsdal 1992, 159).

Bentham's notion of utility has been influential in many disciplines in the social sciences. Since we associate both pain and pleasure with work, both negative and positive incentives are likely to depend on the perceived utility of that job. It is likely that the same incentive can have negative or positive effects, depending on the job, the people, and other factors. In order to design the appropriate incentive structures and working conditions for managers, we need to understand what motivates managers in their work.

In the field of management, textbooks, and articles in professional journals, 'general recipes for employee motivation are as popular as recipes for making gold were in the Middle Ages, but are equally ineffective' (Hofstede 1994b, 25).

What motivates people to work, Hofstede claims, depends on the people and on the work (1972, in 1994b, 25). Hofstede found that effectiveness of incentives may vary according to factors such as age, education, occupation, and gender (1972, in 1994b). Some researchers have found that the validity of the universal motivation theories varies across cultures. An extensive review can be found in Ronen (1986), updated in Deresky (1997). What motivates thus seems to depend on gender, age, occupation, in some situations, and on the home nationality of the managers in others.

Comparative studies, however, have mostly included a small number of countries and were based on poorly matched samples, often difficult to compare. The structural equivalence of municipal CEOs in a large number of countries makes the U.Di.T.E. study a unique data set, the results of which can contribute to management theories of motivation and in the field of comparative management in general, beyond the relevant field in political science. From information about how city managers perceive their ideal job, we can learn about what attracts people to the job, what makes them stay in it, and what perhaps makes them perform the job with enthusiasm. Do people seek this job because of a desire to influence local developments or because they wish to work closely with politicians? To what extent are they similar and different from people who seek jobs as managers in other organizational settings?

Motivational Theory

Motivation can be associated with the choice of behavior and the impetus with which people engage in their job. Motivation can thus be understood as a result of variables deriving from a combination of individual needs, value systems, and environmental conditions (Ronen 1986, 136). If we combine this understanding with our municipal managers, figure 5.3 describes the relationship between the attitudinal and behavioral variables relevant to the CEOs' motivational process. The model allows us, furthermore, to elaborate on the relationship between work goals and motivational theories, and we explore whether values associated with work goals can be attributed to the national cultures of the regional elites.

Figure 5.3: Municipal managers' attitudes and behavior relevant to motivational processes.

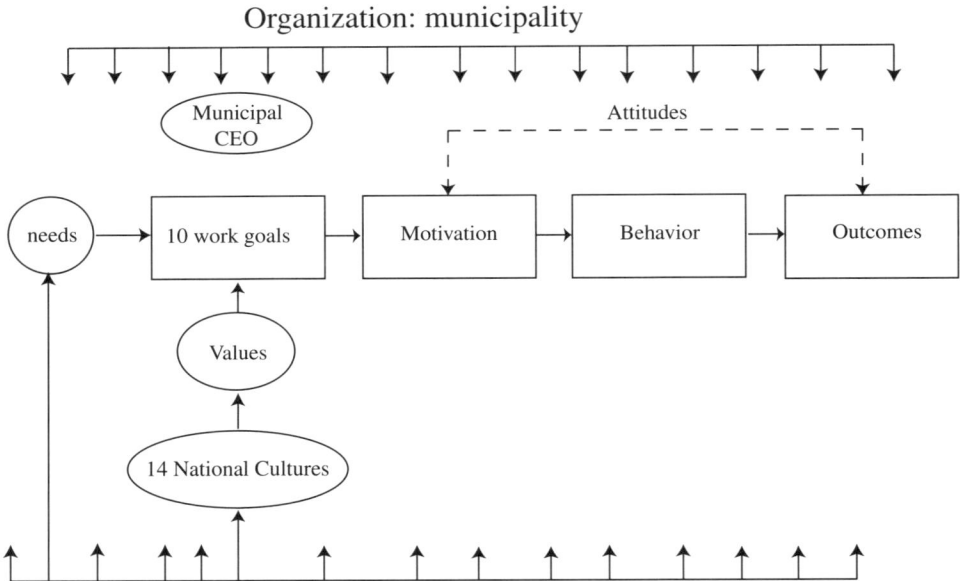

Note: In order to illustrate choices made for this study, we have adopted Ronen's model (1986, 137) of the relationship between the attitudinal and behavioral variables to the individual employee's motivational process.

Assumptions

Following Bentham's notion of utility, motivation theory takes it for granted that it is the prospect of attaining a favorable outcome that motivates an individual to act. Human beings are assumed to be universally need-fulfilling and goal-achieving creatures. The study of work motivation theories furthermore assumes that people strategize behavior that will fulfill their needs and enable them to achieve their goals (Ronen 1986, 136).

In management textbooks, motivation theories are traditionally categorized as content and process theories. Content theories focus on the role of people's needs that are based on attitudes and values. Process theories, on the other hand, deal with the question of how motivated behavior occurs, and how it can be directed (Deresky 1997, 362).

Only an individual can motivate herself or himself. Motivation is understood as an internal process where little is known about how the motivated behavior occurs but more is known indirectly from indicators of motivated behavior in terms of needs and goals.

In this chapter, we will not deal with the psychological mechanism that drives individuals to research positive outcomes. Instead, we focus on specific outcomes that they seek. By studying 'what people want from a job' we get good indicators of valued outcomes and job expectations.

Need Theories and Motivational Models

Among the well-known theories of work motivation we find Maslow's fivefold categorization of needs and Herzberg's two factors of work satisfaction. These theories of work motivation are probably the theories most widely used in comparative studies of different countries. Most of the 38 comparative studies of motivation listed by Ronen examine values and needs, largely replicating, direct or indirect, Maslow's need categories (1986, 157-160). These motivational models will be used in this chapter because of the comparative approach taken by the U.Di.T.E. study, although Hofstede (1980) disputed the universal applicability of Maslow and Herzberg. (We shall see whether Hofstede was right in this argument).

According to Maslow (1946), we are all motivated by certain basic needs, some of which are more fundamental than others. Most fundamental are physiological needs, e.g., food, shelter and sex as well as needs for security. In the middle, we find social needs for rewarding human contacts. At the top is the need for self-actualization, i.e. to realize as fully as possible the potential inherent in us. The hierarchy of the needs implies that needs at lower levels are active motivators, only because they are to some extent satisfied and the next higher level need takes over. A satisfied need is no longer an active motivator.

Herzberg's two-factor theory of motivation categorizes factors that are intrinsic to the job itself, such as achievement, recognition, and advancement, and the theory is believed to represent needs that motivate people to do a better job. Extrinsic factors such as work conditions, job relations, and salary do not act as strong motivators. Extrinsic factors simply maintain a level of satisfaction or dissatisfaction for the person involved (Deresky 1997, 363).

In the European research context of this book, it may be interesting to find that the ideas of Maslow and Herzberg had already been formulated by a Dutch Jesuit priest called Kuylaars, who according to Hofstede (1996, 91) distinguished between external and internal productivity of labour. External productivity was based on the amount of goods and services produced, while internal productivity related to human development and self-actualization. This chapter therefore follows a long-established European tradition of combining the two models in motivation theory.

Methods of Data Collection Applied in the Field of Work Motivation

Herzberg used interview data to construct a model of work motivation. He interviewed accountants and engineers in several American firms. The interviews focused on critical incidents, where strong feelings were involved in a work situation. By this token, Herzberg identified a number of factors, i.e. 'recognition', 'earnings', 'management', and so on.

In the 1960s, Hofstede developed these issues into survey questions for IBM where attitude surveys were carried out as part of a company concern about employee morale (Hofstede 1996, 98). The questionnaire included issues of work goals, e.g., 'how important would it be for you to have a good working relationship with your direct superior?', issues of general beliefs, e.g., 'competition among employees usually does more harm than good', perceptions of organizational climate, e.g., 'how often do you feel nervous or tense at work?' as well as preferences for decision-making style of manager, e.g., authoritarian or consultative style.

The focus in this chapter is on questions regarding work goals. Herzberg's factors were used to formulate questions about the ideal work situation. Respondents were asked to think of the ideal job, disregarding the present job, and were asked to state the importance of, e.g., time for personal or family life when choosing an ideal job. The salience of each factor was described on a 5-point scale. Mean scores were calculated for each goal and each occupation.

VSM 1994 (Hofstede 1994c) is a questionnaire developed for comparing culturally determined values between people from two or more countries and regions. The questionnaire is a result of a development from the original IBM survey questionnaire based on a series of replications. Results from both the IBM and the VSM 1994 questionnaires will be presented below. Table 5.2. shows the goals and how they were formulated in the questionnaire.

In the following, the rank order of the work goals is based on the mean scores. The highest ranking goal has the lowest mean score.

Work Goals of CEOs

The sample of two large multi-country studies on work goals differed with respect to education and employment category. Hofstede's IBM population worked for a

Table 5.2: Work goals and questionnaire items.

Work Goals	Questionnaire Items
personal time	having a job which leaves you sufficient time for your personal or family life
freedom	having considerable freedom to adopt your own approach to the job
challenge	having challenging work to do - work from which you can achieve some personal sense of accomplishment
training	having training opportunities to improve your skills or learn new skills
physical conditions	having good physical working conditions (VSM 94 identical)
use of skills	fully use your skills and abilities on the job
earnings	having an opportunity for high earnings
recognition	getting the recognition you deserve when you do a good job
achievement	having an opportunity to advance to higher level jobs
manager	having good working relationships with your direct superior
cooperation	working with people who cooperate well with each other
living area	living in an area desirable to you and your family
security	having a security that you will be able to work for your company as long as you want; VSM 94: have security of employment
influence development	possibility of influencing developments, make a contribution
politicians	working closely with politicians
consulted	being consulted by your direct superior in his/her decision
advancement	having an opportunity for advancement to higher level jobs
variety and adventure	having an element of variety and adventure in the job

Source: (Hofstede 1991, 51-52, 81-82; VSM 94; U.Di.T.E. Questionnaire).

private, profit-driven organization. Hoppe's sample (1992) consisted of national elites working in leadership roles in academia, government, media, and non-profit driven organizations.

If we focus on the research and development professionals in the IBM study, mostly people with Ph.D. degrees, we match the national elites that Hoppe studied in terms of higher education (Hofstede 1980). Comparing the importance of work goals between the IBM research and development respondents and the national elites (Hofstede 1980; Hoppe 1992) we find a very similar ranking. Reference is made to table 5.3, where we list only the relative ranking of work goals represented in all studies compared here.

For all groups, the most important work goals are challenge, freedom, and working relationship with the manager as well as cooperation. We also find a similar ranking of the least important work goals such as working for a prestigious organization, employment security, and good physical working conditions.

The U.Di.T.E. sample also includes respondents with a higher education. According to table 5.3., the U.Di.T.E. ranking of the work goals does not differ very much from the Hofstede groups and Hoppe groups. Most important goal was 'having a good working relationship with the superior', referred to as 'manager' in the table, although in the case of municipal CEOs the immediate superior is typically the mayor. Additional important goals are cooperation with other people, sufficient personal time, and the possibility of making a contribution.

Advancement seems to be a relatively less important work goal for the city managers than for the Hofstede group. Overall, the city managers of the U.Di.T.E. study seem to have a preference for social goals. The Hofstede and Hoppe samples valued goals regarding the job content higher, (e.g., freedom to adopt own approach to working situation and challenging work).

From the findings of city managers of the U.Di.T.E. study, we rank the four least important goals as: working closely with politicians, employment security, advancement opportunities, and good physical working conditions. This ranking is similar to that of the other groups.

Table 5.3: Work goal importance among IBM R&D professional, national and regional elites.

CC (1967-73) R&D professionals		SSAS (1983-84) National elites from 15 countries		U.Di.T.E. (1996-97) Regional elites from 14 countries	
Rank	Most Important	Rank	Most Important	Rank	Most Important
1	manager	1	manager	1	manager
2	cooperation	2	cooperation	2	cooperation
3	advancement	3	make a contribution	3	personal time
4	personal time	4	personal time	4	make a contribution
5	make a contribution	5	advancement	5	advancement
6	security	6	physical working conditions	6	physical working conditions
7	physical working conditions	7	security	7	security

Source: Hoppe 1992, 22.

(): Period of data collection. CC: Cultures Consequences; SSAS: Salzburg Seminar Aulumni/ae Study, U.Di.T.E.

Values of Local Government CEOs in Job Motivation

If we consider some additional work goals, besides the ones listed in table 5.3., we find that the differences in ranking suggest that we should categorize the work goals according to some need categories. Some of the work goals touch on the content of the jobs, e.g., 'training', 'challenge', 'freedom', 'up-to-datedness', 'use of skills', 'influence on the development', as well as 'variety' and 'adventure'. Other goals are personal goals such as 'advancement', 'recognition', 'earnings'. Some goals can be categorized as social goals, e.g., 'cooperation', 'manager', and 'family'. Finally, some goals relate to the living and working environment such as 'contribution to the company', 'efficient department', 'security', 'living area', 'benefits', 'working conditions', and 'successful company'.

Work Goals of Public and Private Managers

If we compare the private and the local public managers, we find a similar difference in the ranking of work goals among the four most important ones. First and second line managers from the IBM cooperation rank job content goals such as challenge and freedom highest. City managers rank social needs higher, such as cooperation and good relations with the manager (mayor). Please refer to table 5.4.

Table 5.4: The four most important goals of IBM and city managers.

Work Goals	City Managers 14 Western Countries (N = 4440)	First and Second Line IBM Managers 15 European Countries (N = 4000; Hofstede 1972)
High (self-actualization and esteem needs)		
Challenge		1
Freedom		2
Influence development	3	
Work with politicians		
Variety and adventure		
Advancement		
Middle (social Needs)		
Cooperation	1	3, 4
Manager	2	3, 4
Consulted		
Personal time	4	
Low (security and physiological needs)		
Security		
Physical conditions		

These findings suggest that social goals are important issues related to the job as city manager, and that there are indeed differences in terms of work goals. One contribution to an understanding of the importance of 'social needs' for managers is that a good working relationship with the mayor (represented by the term 'manager' in the table) is crucial for municipal CEOs.

Work Goals of City Managers in Western Countries in a Comparative Perspective

If we compare the national samples of the U.Di.T.E. study, the social goals seem to be ranked highest, except in the case of the Finnish and Spanish samples of city managers. Social needs is one of three need categories constructed on the basis of a simple index, adding the average responses to the questionnaire and dividing by the number of questions contained in the appropriate need category. For simplicity, the assumption is that each question of a need category is of equal importance in all countries of the U.Di.T.E. study. The ego need category is a simple addition of variation and adventure, advancement, contribution and working closely with politicians. The social need category is a simple addition of 'cooperation', 'manager', 'personal time' and the importance of being 'consulted'. The basic need category is a simple addition of the importance of 'physical conditions' and 'security'. (See table 5.2 above for the exact wording of the work goals).

Table 5.5: Rank order of ego, social, and basic needs of city managers in 14 western countries.

Country	EGO-needs	Rank	SOCIAL-needs	Rank	BASIC-needs	Rank
Fin	1,99	1	2,40	2	2,61	3
N	2,40	2	1,87	1	2,72	3
S	2,28	2	1,90	1	2,51	3
DK	2,06	2	1,83	1	2,82	3
UK	2,17	2	1,97	1	2,67	3
IRL	2,08	2	1,77	1	2,29	3
NL	2,38	2	1,96	1	2,51	3
B	2,56	3	2,00	1	2,40	2
F	2,41	2	2,07	1	2,67	3
I	2,59	3	1,94	1	2,28	2
E	2,84	3	1,90	2	1,87	1
P	2,12	3	1,74	1	1,80	2
USA	2,19	2	1,84	1	2,40	3
AUS	2,28	2	1,75	1	2,39	3

Note: Mean scores of 2001-10. 1 utmost importance, 5 no or little importance.

Values of Local Government CEOs in Job Motivation

Table 5.6: The five most important goals by country.

Needs	Fin	Nor	Swe	Den	UK	Irl	Nl	Bel	Fra	Ita	Spa	Por	USA	AUS
ego														
variety & adventure		2	1	1	1	5	3	4	1			5	4	5
advancement						2			5	2				
contribution	3		4	4	2	3							3	3
politicians														
social														
cooperation	1	3	3	5	5	4	1	1	4	1	1	2	5	4
manager	2	1	2	2	3	1	2	2	2	4	4	1	1	1
personal time	4	5					4	3			2	4	2	2
consulted		4	5	3	4		5	5	3	5				
basic														
physical conditions										3	5			
security	5									3	4			

In seven countries (Finland, Sweden, Denmark, the UK, Ireland, USA, and Australia), the work goal of making a 'contribution' ranked among the four most important goals according to table 5.6.

The ranking of goals according to table 5.7 suggests that goals regarding the content of the job as well as working conditions are listed as the least important goals. As for the job-content goals, the least important goal is the possibility of working with politicians. This is clearly the case in all countries except Denmark, the Netherlands, and Norway. Further country findings will have to be used to explain why these countries deviate here.

Conclusion

Analysis of the U.Di.T.E. findings regarding work goals suggests that social needs are the most important goals associated with the job as a city manager. The preference for social goals is supported by findings in the U.Di.T.E. study regarding general beliefs, e.g., it is unfortunate to be poor, sick, and old. The importance of social issues may prove to be a differentiating characteristic of this type of manager. More analyses are needed to substantiate this point.

The cross-cultural findings regarding work goals of city managers are valuable since work values of regional public elites in European countries have become

Table 5.7: The five least important goals by country.

Needs	Fin	Nor	Swe	Den	UK	Irl	Nl	Bel	Fra	Ita	Spa	Por	USA	AUS
ego														
var & adv	5									3	2			
advancement	3	1	4	1	4		1	2	5		5	5	2	4
contribution		5					5	4		5	3	3		
politicians	1	2	1	5	1	1	3	1	1	1	1	1	1	1
social														
cooperation														
manager														
personal time			5	4	5	5			3	4				
consulted	4					4					4	2	5	5
basic physical conditions														
	2	3	2	3	2	3	4	5	4		4	3	3	3
security		4	3	2	3	2	2	3	2	2		4		2

Note: Among the least important work goals, 1) is the most important goal relative to other goals indicated by each national sample of munipical CEOs. Among least important goals, 5) is the least important.

increasingly relevant as the political and economic internationalization of Europe develops. The public sector at the regional level becomes exposed to more than one national culture. The public sector has been exposed to the importance of management ideas, and new organizational methods have developed not only in private organizations, but also in different national contexts.

For the process of introducing such streamlining and internationalizing organizational development, it would be fruitful to find the origin of the current fundamental attitudes towards key issues of the public work situation: Who decides how much and how? To what extent should work processes be standardized by rules? And how do we motivate subordinates to work more efficiently and with more satisfaction?

Assistance in making a value profile of local government top civil servants could perhaps be obtained by looking for research results from fields beyond the traditional political science field. Such a field is international and comparative management, where the study subject of large international private business organizations for a long time has faced similar demands from an increasingly international environment.

Overall, our analysis shows that all the work goals of European local government

CEOs indicate a very strong social interest and commitment to the social welfare of the local community. The care for the unfortunate, poor, sick, old, or unemployed is one of the additional indicators of a strong commitment to social welfare. As expected, regional elites from countries with a long tradition for welfare policy, such as Sweden, Finland, Denmark and the Netherlands, have higher preferences for social issues than do regional elites from Portugal, Italy and France and Spain.

Practical Consequences

There are at least two points to be made as to the practical consequences of these findings. First, the transfer of management ideas from other cultural situations cannot be done easily without adjustment. Decentralization is not likely to work well without adjustment in high power countries. Decentralization requires that the subordinate is at ease openly speaking her/his mind to the boss, even in disagreement. In such situations, the manager should establish a formal structure of participation where the subordinate feels entitled to say that two and two is four, even when the subordinate knows that the boss thinks that the result is five.

The fact that decentralization comes more easily to members of low power distance countries is illustrated by the findings that decentralization in local governments has taken place to a larger extent in countries with a low power distance culture than in high power countries. Furthermore, result-based incentives are unlikely to work well without adjustment in local governments in all 14 countries because of the generally low masculinity score for the whole population. The most sophisticated adjustment is likely to be required in Sweden, Finland, Denmark and the Netherlands, because the city managers of these countries score extremely low on masculinity.

Our findings show that the four dimensions meaningfully describe work-related value differences between national groups of local government CEOs. A second practical consequence is that the Hofstede framework will be useful for city managers in preparing for the cross-cultural encounters which, following the process of internationalization, will inevitably increase in number and intensity.

CHAPTER 6

Playing by the Rules in Portuguese Local Government: Interpretations of the Discourse of Administrative Leadership

BY JOSÉ PINHEIRO NEVES AND JOEL FELIZES

This study attempts to extend research on local government through an interpretation of the agents' discourse. By partially drawing on Anthony Giddens' perspective (Giddens 1984), we assume that discourse is built into the relation between the everyday conduct of municipal chief administrative officers (CAO) (and its respective rationalization) and the broader context where this *action* takes place. This means that we search for an empirical ground in the agents' *subjectivity*. This search has two implications: first, there is a departure from strict positivist or functionalist approaches; second, this demarcation is supported by a method that, being necessarily malleable, is at the same time aware of its uncertainty.

Rationalities, Power Relations and the Organization

Traditional social scientific theories tend to gravitate between structures or systems on the one hand, and individuals bearing rational strategies on the other. This discourse thus tends to favour the idea of integration, of an individual and a social reproduction that unites society and (in an indirect manner) scientific discourse itself. A possible starting point for a different perspective would be to assume the importance of the mechanisms behind that reproduction, the process by which *meaning* is produced.

The concept of bureaucracy is a good example of this argument: the bureaucratic organization is often simplified in order to symbolize a kind of machine that generates dysfunctions, partly due to the actors' strategies (Merton 1949; Selznick 1949; Gouldner 1954; Crozier 1964), or, in a somewhat opposite interpretation, a machine that simply generates a neutral framework for the above mentioned societal or organizational integration (Woodward 1965; Pugh *et al.* 1969; Perrow 1972). A common scientific strategy uses both perspectives in an effort to improve the efficiency and transparency of bureaucratic organizations expecting to eliminate their *neurotic* potential. The problem is that the scientist usually sees himself becoming either an instrument or an *academic* outsider for the reproduction of that bureaucracy. A possible alternative to this instrumentalization would be a stronger concern with epistemological and theoretical problematization, avoiding an excessive belief in its effective impact and assuming the humble and hermeneutic status of scientific work.

In the more specific context of local administration, it is necessary to sustain a perspective that is aware of the presence of multiple frameworks. This awareness results from the combination of theoretical and empirical sources. Thus, we argue that ideas, such as those derived from Anthony Giddens' theory of structuration (Giddens 1984) and from the French post-structuralism (Foucault 1983; Deleuze & Guattari 1988) can be quite illuminating, since finding more or less evident features in the context under consideration is interpreted in order to privilege their relative condition, in the sense that those features are not only malleable but also reflect local signs of an inescapable relational context.

Our particular concern with the administrative structuration of local governments does not mean that the presence of a political dimension in such a context can be ignored. Power is here more than an inevitable element derived from the organization's nature. A relational theory of power sees the entire organization as an entity produced and reproduced by a frame of structures and actions embedded in power relations. In addition to this perspective, Michel Foucault (1979) develops a critical argument, stressing the diffuse character of such relations and assuming an overall condition of modern societies and organizations in which people become subjects, in the sense that they are simultaneously 'subjectified' and constituted as isolated individuals.

It could be argued that this perspective prevents the search for a solid empirical basis, since the key concept of power has a diffuse and relational nature. However, what is being suggested is that since power is above all something that creates and shapes structures and actions, research conducted on this basis is not focused on power itself, but on its effects, being the *subjectification* of the actors involved. This means that the separation between a macro and a micro level is quite artificial and that any understanding of the multiple frameworks that involve local governments' administrative personnel requires a methodology which can simultaneously focus on a structural or institutional background and on the agents' strategies, tactics and reactions that reflect dynamics of empowerment and disempowerment, constrained by a more general frame of power relations.

A Brief Remark on the Methodology

The empirical approach we are developing here sees administrative personnel in local governments as engaged in a frame of relations that involve constant exchanges of power. In this sense, to assume that such a group has a stable identity is misleading, since those people face a constant dynamic of relations that involve different purposes or effects, varying from a simple recognition of the role performed by the administrative officer to the search for control over strategic positions.

In an attempt to define patterns in the dynamic identities and strategies within the organization, our perspective aims to combine two rationalities often seen as contenders: the first one usually combines a global strategy with subsequent tactics, while the other tends to be a more confused or ambiguous process. As many recent theories stress, social agents share these two poles of social action. The failure of *technocratic* organizational theories suggested above can thus be seen as an unsuccessful attempt to eliminate *ambiguous* behaviour, wrongly believed as irrational, that was allegedly blocking the organization's efficiency. A first important rupture in this technocratic view is attained by studies that stress organizational ambiguity with regard to technology, decision-making and participation (for an overview see Reed 1985).

Dealing with empirical findings, we assumed that the two rationalities were expressed by municipal CAOs in two different ways: the more calculating rationality, corresponding to their 'discursive consciousness' (Giddens 1984, 7), was particularly evident when CAOs were confronted with the survey conducted in 1996 (see technical appendix) or with the presence of a researcher, as was the case in the interviews conducted between 1991 and 1995 that we also consider relevant for this study. The other *rationality*, more reactive or emotional, more often seeking the immediate effect or benefit, is particularly present in CAOs' everyday actions, corresponds more to their 'practical consciousness' (Giddens 1984, 7), which we tried to capture through a general interpretation of our empirical materials, namely through the crossing of some variables of the survey and through qualitative data (interviews, structured observation) related to that 'everyday action'.

Finally, this study shares some similarities with the one developed by Morten Balle Hansen (see the following chapter), since it also deals with the relation between the *games* concerning organizational rules and the way these games are rationalized and enacted. We consider as crucial a contextual game, played around the general rules that push Portuguese local government into a peripheral position.

The Political-Administrative System Surrounding the CAO

The context surrounding the CAOs' position and rationalities is heavily influenced, on one hand, by the political structure that governs Portuguese local government and, on the other, by the body of legislation that stands as a permanent concern and source of legitimization for the CAOs' activities.

As we try to illustrate in figure 6.1, Portuguese municipalities, despite a 'political status' that grants them relatively high autonomy (elected bodies, financial autonomy, extended duties), have in fact a low 'legal status', in the sense that they see their functions as very limited (Goldsmith 1995, 247). This low legal status can be seen as a consequence of multiple factors, some of them present in local leader's opinions. In fact, they tend to highlight the lack of financial resources and the complexity of bureaucratic procedures as the most important barriers to the development of their policies. The historical context is one of centralization, a tradition that has

Playing by the Rules in Portuguese Local Government

hardly changed under the democratic regime established after 1974. Two examples illustrate our point: first, the recent defeat, by a referendum, of a regionalization project that had the support of a majority of local leaders but which faced a strong opposition in many local communities, directed mainly against the geographic delimitation of the different regions. Second, we find that national leaders, whether in central government or in key positions in political parties, are rarely recruited from among local government leaders. These leaders, if invited to occupy these important positions, tend to be reluctant, preferring to maintain their role as influential persons in their local communities.

Figure 6.1: Political and administrative structures of Portuguese local government.

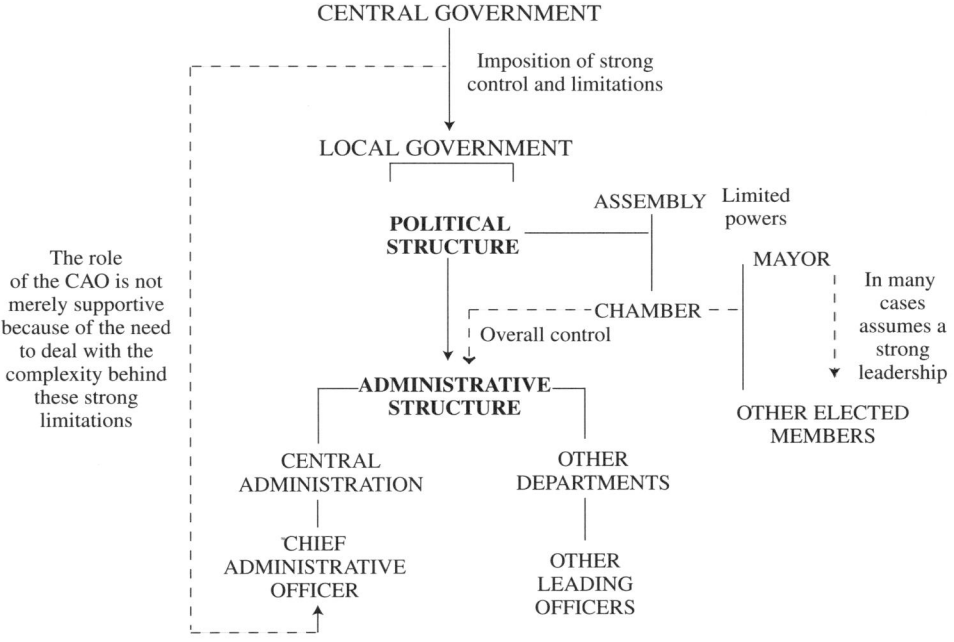

It is important to note that this dependent role played by Portuguese local government is nevertheless crucial to the political struggle involving central and local government relations. The mayor tends to act as an advocate for the local community in its demands. Recent changes in local government legislation have increased the mayor's powers. Thus, the mayor has become the real chief executive officer (CEO) of the municipality, since he is also responsible for the management and direction of human resources, and he has the power to 'change or revoke acts carried out by municipal personnel' (section 2 of Article 53, Act 100/84, amended by Act 18/91). Figure 6.1 highlights this leading role assumed by the mayor; however, since the council (chamber) is elected according to a proportional system (in some cases there is not a single party majority), this leadership is weakened if the mayor faces a hostile and strong opposition.

The administrative structure, being more diversified than what is shown in figure 6.1, is clearly divided into different 'services' or 'departments', each one with its respective hierarchy and usually placed under the overall responsibility of one of the elected members. However, the 'general' or 'central administration' (led by the CAO) is almost always under the mayor's direct supervision. Since the legal framework for the CAO's activity has recently changed, we will present it in more detail.

Until 1984, the administrative functions of Portuguese municipalities were under the responsibility of a chief secretary, a position similar to that of a chief executive officer in other countries. The chief secretary worked under a national board placed under central government control: his status and functions were defined by national administrative law, which was applicable countrywide. This situation began to change after the 1974 democratic revolution, which proclaimed the principles of decentralization and local autonomy.

The administrative structure of Portuguese local governments was thus consolidated between the years 1984 and 1991, though at the expense of a bureaucratic and dispersed legal framework. Briefly, there are three laws (with some additional amendments) that we regard as the most relevant: (1) Act 116/84, a general frame determining the municipal autonomy to organize local administration, revoking the old national board (1936); (2) Act 247/87, defining the careers and recruitment of local government personnel, enacting nominations as the common procedure (this principle was revoked four years later); (3) since the recruitment of leading officers in public administration was regulated in 1989, central government passed Act 198/91, which determined the status of leading administrative personnel placed in municipalities.

Each municipality is to set up and elaborate its own organization and personnel. Thus, the activities of chief administrative officers can vary from one municipality to another. Generally, they participate in the drawing up and carrying out of the municipality's policies and budgets. They also participate in human resource management and supervision and manage organizations that belong to the general directorate of the department, division or area under the authority of the mayor (or other councillors). National law also determines a somewhat unstable position for CAOs, for these professionals must be recruited on a temporary basis (three years, but renewable). These contracts, known as 'commissions of service', are equivalent to others for leading personnel in public administration.

That we are dealing with a confused legal framework can be confirmed if we recall that Act 116/84, the first attempt to reorganize local governments' technical and administrative services, has been amended in various articles, many of them changed seventeen months later (Act 44/85).[1] Furthermore, the regulations for recruiting

---

[1] An important change from Act 116/84 to Act 44/85 relates to the financial situation of the chief administrative officers: instead of earning up to 50% of their basic wage from their function as notary in municipalities' contracts, the limit was increased up to 70%. Recently, some CAOs lost this privilege, as their mayors interpreted this 'private' notary public as irregular.

technical or administrative personnel are dispersed in several laws, as in many cases national laws were later (but only partially) adapted to the municipal context.

There is indeed an interesting outcome of this legal *jumble*: in 1991, recognizing the persistence of irregular recruitment and promotion in many municipalities, the government passed a law (Act 413/91, amended in 1992) that prescribed severe financial punishments for any future violations. Elected members are now personally responsible for any undue payments made to personnel who have been irregularly recruited or promoted.

In a general appraisal, chief administrative officers, based on their financial and mainly legislative knowledge, control an important resource: the interpretation of rules. So, it is not evident, as some CAOs maintain, that their importance is decreasing. As one of our interviewees explained:

> My duty is to execute and to decide ... I mean, I decide (...) in terms of giving legal advice so that the elected bodies may decide; furthermore, I decide on the administrative queries that may occur, like when licensing private buildings' construction: the officer asks me if a certain project needs the municipality's permission, or if any other entity should be consulted – there I'm the one who decides, I must say 'it has to be done this or that way' (...) When there is doubt about a promotion, I'll have to decide.

If the CAO can be seen as a disempowered agent in the whole local government *game*, we must recognize that he is nevertheless a relevant *player*, as he uses his resources (mainly control over important rules) in order to mediate parts of the relations between local government and other agents.

According to Pierre Grémion, there is a local political-administrative system that connects the external and the organizational contexts through 'relays' (mediating brokers). Thus, 'permanent networks are structured around some *relays* who become crucial in the organization's concrete action' (Grémion 1976, 12). In this context, it is possible to understand the CAO as a special type of relay (see figure 6.1): operating in the core of the bureaucratic structure, maintaining a permanent relation with external agents, supporting many of the decisions made by the political structure.

Between Rules and Rationalization: the Chameleonic CAO

In the previous section we focused on the institutional arrangements relevant to the position occupied by chief administrative officers. Here we wish to emphasize that the impact of the *formal* context varies according to certain characteristics of the CAOs, including the way they rationalize a whole set of rules and relations that constitute the everyday activity of these professionals.

A central variable for the characterization of Portuguese CAOs is their educational background. As we show in table 6.1, this background is strongly influenced by the CAOs' age. This is explained by a more general cause: Portugal saw the global educational level increasing, particularly in the last two decades.

Table 6.1: Age 'versus' educational background of Portuguese CAOs %. (N = 102).

	Years in school				
Age	6 - 9	10 - 12	13 or more	Total	N
29 - 42	3	11	86	100	36
43 - 52	25	43	33	100	40
53 - 67	42	35	23	100	26
Total	22	29	49	100	102

Total chi^2 = 33,865; probability of non-association: less than 0.0001.
Source: U.Di.T.E. survey. Two respondents did not answer one or both of the questions.

We see in table 6.1 the difference between a younger generation, more educated, and the older CAOs, who surely did not have the same opportunities to go to the university: Among the CAOs 43 years or older, only 21% has university degrees (not displayed) and only 29% had more than 13 years of full-time education (19 out of 66).

Most of the CAOs are in their current position for a few years (the average is between four and five years), independently of their age or educational background. This finding reflects the above-mentioned recent transformation in the formal structures of local government. It may also have an overall influence on the CAOs' attitude toward their jobs (in many cases a new post obtained after a long career in local administration), an attitude that reveals a tension between the desire to introduce changes and the importance of acting according to the rules. This orientation to rules is also related to the above-mentioned dependent role played by Portuguese local government, but here seen in a more indirect manner. In order to understand the attitude of CAOs, we should remember that their position in local administration is closely related to the control over legislative knowledge. In Portugal, a particularly complex body of legislation is applicable to local administration: this is so because there has been a constant increase in local government duties, there are new rules deriving from the use of European funding, and there are national laws that need to be interpreted in the specific frame of local administration. Underlying this complexity, we again find the strong presence of the State (typical in non-advanced capitalist economies), that generates a global dependence of civil society toward the public institutions and thus requires control over the activities that involve the use of public resources.

The Powerful Rule
During our research, one of our recurring difficulties was the uniform attitude of chief administrative officers toward the legislation with which they have to deal

every day. This attitude can be summarized in the statement of one of our interviewees: 'in the good pursuit of my duties, first of all, it is necessary to have a profound knowledge of the legislation that rules us. Without a profound knowledge, one can't go very far'. Thus, we think of this attitude as a riddle, laying its solution possibly on the variation behind that common statement. In other words, a general concern with a very complex problem (the mentioned legal jumble), is probably rationalized by our agents in different ways.

We find a first source of diversity in the work routine of a CAO: it consists of a series of diversified and often brief contacts with many persons in order to deal with legal problems. However, this activity can be somewhat chaotic (from the CAO point of view). As the above-mentioned interviewee stated, 'there are many circumstances that really disturb the action. There are many problems that appear when I'm not expecting them. The unexpected, the difficulty in predicting what may happen during the day, raises difficulties and forces me to change the plans I've made in the beginning'. Another CAO wrote a specific note in the survey stressing the variety and adventure contained in her job. There seems to exist a daily tension for the CAO, opposing the 'unexpected' events and the attempt to control them.

The priority that CAOs attribute to the knowledge of legislation is probably the solution they find for that tension. When confronted with a (hypothetical) concrete situation that demands a rating between three possible strategies (see table 6.2), 68% of the Portuguese CAOs prefer to comply with established rules and procedures.

One of the CAOs we interviewed used the image of the 'traffic warden' to illustrate his role. It is somewhat similar to the concept of 'relay' used above. In a context where rules become pre-eminent, the task of keeping the flow of rules in a sustainable status, avoiding accidents (violations) gains new importance.

Table 6.2: First priority given to different forms of dealing with a situation that demands a choice, in per cent (N = 100).

Possible strategy	*CAOs who mention it as first priority %*
Observing the established rules and procedures (e.g., laws, regulations and internal procedures)	68
Accomplishing tasks efficiently and quickly	19
Ensuring that all those involved with decision-making are satisfied with the decision-making processes and their outcome	13
Total	100

Source: U.Di.T.E. survey. Four respondents did not answer the question.

However, there are always margins of uncertainty, situations that show that these bureaucratic organizations are also, to a certain extent, 'loosely coupled systems' (March & Olsen 1989). The body of legislation can be interpreted in different manners. There are also circumstances where a rigid application of legal principles could endanger the organization's stability.

This seems to be the case with the employees' assessment (one of the duties of CAOs and other leading officers of the same rank). There are four possible grades (insufficient, sufficient, good and very good), but in fact CAOs adopt a criterion that in reality neutralizes the purpose of this assessment: they give the 'insufficient' or even the 'sufficient' mark to an employee only in exceptional situations, oscillating between the 'good' and the 'very good'. As one of the CAOs stated, 'In conclusion, good is the normal measure. It is what we want here, otherwise it would be a calamity.'

There is a difference between giving priority to the observation of rules and admitting that these rules can be broken. Hence, table 6.3 shows that in spite of being divided about the importance of keeping the rules, a sizable proportion of our respondents believe that no employee in the organization should ever break the rules (45%, whereas 55% express some doubts or disagree). Confronting this result with the variable 'educational background', we notice that the two most significant clusters are in opposite positions: on one hand, we have those who are more *educated* and tend to be less rigid about the possibility of breaking rules (32%); on the other hand, we find those 28% of CAOs who spent less years in school and who emphasize that rules should never be broken.

Table 6.3: Compliance to rules versus years of education. %

	Rules of an organization should not be broken - not even when the employee thinks it is in the best interest of the organization			
Years of full-time education	Totally agree	Other answers	Total	N
From 6 to 12 years	55	45	100	51
13 years or more	35	65	100	49
Totals:	45	55	100	100

Total chi^2 = 4,123; probability of non-association: 0.042.
Source: U.Di.T.E. survey. Four respondents did not answer one or both of the questions.

This result helps us to clarify how organizational rules are dealt with in the everyday activities of chief administrative officers. Our argument is that there is a possible difference between those who tend to assimilate the importance of formal rules versus those who maintain a certain 'discursive' distance toward the rules. Of course, part of the explanation for this finding lies in the meaning of the word 'rule'. Here we will assume a twofold meaning, as Giddens also suggests: 'it is commonly taken for granted among social scientists that the more abstract rules – e.g., codified law – are the most influential in the structuring of social activity. I would propose, however, that many seemingly trivial procedures followed in daily life have a more profound influence upon the generality of social conduct' (1984, 22).

In the case of the CAOs who reveal a strict attitude, we suggest that they tend to mix those intensive and informal rules with the formalized and strongly sanctioned ones. That is, a more *severe* CAO tends to support his practice (i.e. the way he follows organizational regulations and conduct, particularly those that mediate his relation with others, such as language and conversation rules) assuming that not only legal rules but also many other tacit rules have a formalized and strongly sanctioned nature. The apparently liberal CAO who does not penalize the employees is somehow replacing a rule by a new and also rigid one ('otherwise it would be a calamity'). It is also important to note that part of the work methods in these administrative departments were introduced by the CAO: again, a more severe CAO may be quite proud of his work and prohibit any violation of the rules he has partly formulated.

In the case of the less rigid CAOs with a higher educational background, they seem to extend the way they follow formal rules to the *iceberg* of informal rules. They play with a larger margin of uncertainty, possibly thinking that rules need not be followed or that there are indeed different interpretations of a rule.

The Modernist Discourse of Local Administration

We shall now highlight another aspect of CAOs' discourse: namely, how they perceive their role as persons involved in possible changes that may affect local government. What we note is that almost all CAOs are in favour of the implementation of important changes: survey results show that they praise organizational change, that they value the employees' participation and find the development of new routines and work methods important or very important in their daily activity. Many CAOs also find their job quite attractive: as one CAO told us, 'knowing the persons, the elected members with whom we work, the place where we work (…) knowing *every little corner of the house*, all this is more than enough to justify why I'm not attracted to any other job'.

CAOs thus seem to be perfectly integrated in what we could term the modern *image* of local administration. This discursive rationalization, allowing these professionals 'to present themselves as active, modern managers' (Costa *et al.* 1998, 222), is depicted in table 6.4. We compared CAOs' attitude toward reorganization with their educational background, not in order to reveal an association between the variables, but to instead demonstrate the non-association. A majority of the CAOs clearly sustain the need to reorganize local administration (60%, opposed to the 7% that we count as holding a conservative position), independently of their educational background (or of their age, since these two variables are closely related).

Table 6.4: Attitude toward the need for reorganization 'versus' education. %

Years of full-time education	Totally agree %	*The need for change and reorganization of the local government sector has been greatly exaggerated*		Total
		Partly agree or undecided %	Disagree or strongly disagree %	
Until 12 years	6	37	58	100
13 years or more	8	30	62	100
Total	7	33	60	100

Total chi^2 = 0.591; probability of non-association: 0.7442.
Source: U.Di.T.E. survey. Two respondents missing.

At first glance, these results are not consistent with the previously emphasized over-estimation of the rules. However, more than a contradiction between what CAOs say and do, there is an effective tension on their discursive consciousness, oscillating between two poles: one, the ideal image of their role and of the need to change the rules of the game (e.g., the struggle for de-bureaucratization); the other, an image brought on by their practical consciousness, by their everyday action, pushing them toward the reproduction and constant surveillance of the rules (formal or informal).

Figure 6.2: Contexts for the articulation of practical and discursive consciousness.

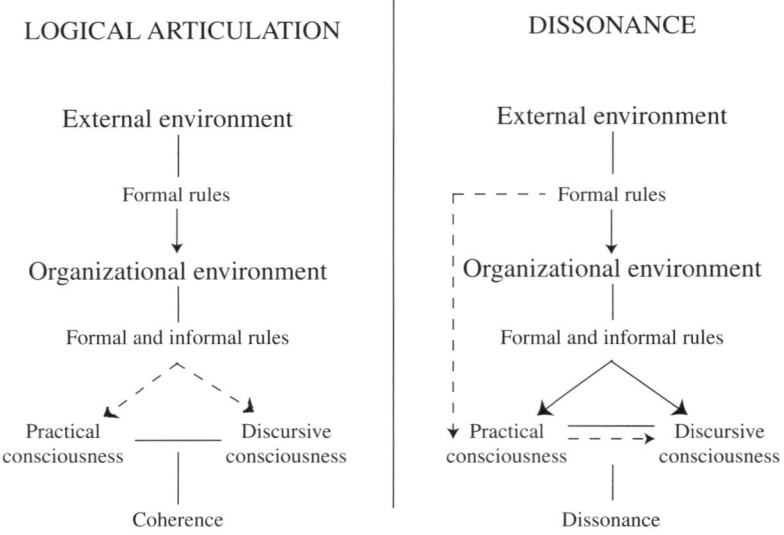

This discursive *dissonance*, sketched out on the right side of figure 6.2, can also be seen as a consequence of the prevailing discourse in the organizational environment (which is a decisive source for the CAOs socialization, as most of them worked their way up through the ranks of public administration). As officers in leading roles, CAOs also represent their local government, they know 'every little corner of the house'. Thus, CAOs are consonant with the modernist discourse of local government, which highlights the demand for more power to local government and the general belief that a reform of the entire public administration system is needed.

Nevertheless, many of the changes introduced in local government ended in more legislation and tighter rules, resembling what Michel Crozier (1964) termed the 'vicious circle' of bureaucracy. Thus, the modernist discourse that CAOs adopt tends to confirm Giddens's idea that: there are obvious sources of tension between practical consciousness (constant surveillance over rules) and discursive consciousness (the modernist discourse).

Conclusion

In this study, we suggested that research on local government should focus on the hermeneutic character of social science, stressing that 'the discovery of (...) generalizations (...) is only one concern among others that are equally important to the theoretical content of social science. Chief among these other concerns is the provision of conceptual means for analysing what actors know about why they act as they do' (Giddens 1984, xix). Observing the relation between chief administrative officers' discourse and its context, we then searched for those conceptual means, through the analysis of survey and interviews' results.

The survey presented a stimulating challenge to us: some of the results revealed the specificity of the Portuguese case, particularly the fact that CAOs, in their everyday activities, attach great importance (more than in any other of the countries where the survey was conducted), to following established rules and procedures. Embedded in the local political-administrative system, the CAO is a special type of relay (see figure 6.1), operating in the core of the bureaucratic structure and maintaining a permanent relation with external agents, (legally) supporting many of the decisions made by the political structure.

As we approach the organizational environment, we find the CAO as an agent deeply concerned with the observation of rules, assuming the role of 'traffic warden'. This led us to clarify how organizational rules are dealt with in the everyday action of chief administrative officers. As Giddens explains, 'the discursive formulation of a rule is already an interpretation of it, that may in itself alter the form of its application' (1984, 22-23). This point deserves clarification. In fact, Giddens follows Ludwig Wittgenstein's conception of the 'language game'. According to Jürgen Habermas, this conception 'determines the use of the linguistic expressions, not as the result of individual teleological actions on the part of isolated, purposively acting subjects but as the 'common behaviour of mankind." Moreover, 'the network of activities and speech acts is constituted by an antecedent accord about an intersubjectively shared form of life, or by a preunderstanding of a common practice regulated by institutions and customs' (1995, 63). Given the language game behind the use of the term 'rule', there is a possible difference between CAOs who tend to assimilate the importance of formal and informal rules versus those who maintain a certain 'discursive' distance toward the rules. This difference is rather subtle, but it shows a possible fracture between more and less conservative CAOs.

The other result that we found in agreement with the overvaluation of rules is the fact that almost all CAOs are in favour of implementing major organizational changes: survey results show that they value the employees' participation in this change and that they find the development of new routines and work methods important or very important in their daily activity. We interpret these attitudes as a global effect of CAOs' organizational socialization, of an environment characterized by a unanimous discourse that praises the need to modernize local administration.

More than an ornament, this perception of being a modern manager is an important ingredient in the mediation between CAOs' practical and discursive consciousness. They stand at a peripheral position in the whole political game, facing the tension between the need to keep playing the game (as members of the local government's *modernist brotherhood*) and the obligation to play it with their own means. CAOs must be the guardians of the rules' temple.

CHAPTER 7

Actors, Structures, and Rules: the Life of Danish CEOs

BY MORTEN BALLE HANSEN

Introduction

> No end of trouble has been brought about by the tendency of philosophers to presume that the question 'What is X doing?' has a unitary answer; ... For it soon becomes apparent that there are many possible responses to such a question: someone may be said to be 'bringing down a metal implement on wood', 'chopping logs', 'doing his job', 'having fun', etc. ... all these characterizations can be quite correct descriptions of what is going on – although, depending upon the context in which the query is formulated, only certain of them will be 'appropriate' [Giddens 1993, 87].

The literature on managerial work offers numerous descriptions of managerial behaviour (Carlson 1951; Mintzberg 1973; Stewart 1982). Colin Hales (1986; 1993) provides an illuminating review of many of these descriptions under the heading of 'form' and 'content', while Tony Watson (1994) has written an eminently ethnographic 'search for management'. The behavioural tradition has been criticized for being atheoretical (Fondas & Stewart 1994; Hales 1986; Mintzberg 1991), for ignoring the managers' embeddedness in institutional settings (Willmott 1987) and for a number of other 'failures'. This chapter addresses some of these issues. A conceptual framework for analyzing the structuration of managerial work from an institutional actor-structure perspective is elaborated and applied to a case study of the work of Danish municipal CEOs. The three most important methods were structured observations of fifteen Danish CEOs, semi-structured interviews with the same fifteen CEOs and a survey of all Danish CEOs. The structured observations were basically a replication of Mintzberg's study of managerial work (1973) with two important adjustments. Inspired by a suggestion by Martinko & Gardner (1985), the importance of the particular social context and an interest in the meaning of the interaction for the actors were emphasized in order to provide 'thick' description (Geertz 1973).

The study shares an interest in some basic questions from the behavioral research tradition: What do managers do? Why do managers act the way they do? How can managers shape their organizations and environments? However, these questions are addressed with the institutional embeddedness of managerial behavior in mind. Theoretically, the study is informed by the actor-structure debate in the social sciences (Giddens 1984; Mouzelis 1995), by the New Institutionalism in organizational research (March & Olsen 1989; Powell & DiMaggio 1991) as well as by the abovementioned behavioural tradition within management research. The study is based on the premise that it is important to 'bring society back in' (Friedland & Alford 1991) to management research in order to understand the behaviour of managers.

The Conceptual Framework

The theoretical framework is based on the rather conventional assumption that society and its organizations are kept alive by human beings. Our understanding of managers and their organizations must therefore be based on some assumptions concerning why humans act the way they do.

Human action is conceived of as structured by '*cultural rules*' (Meyer, Boli & Thomas 1987) in numerous ways. These cultural rules provide meaning and value to particular social units and actions and integrate these in larger social systems of meaning and interaction. Cultural rules are both enabling and constraining for particular social actors (Giddens 1984). Rules can be more or less extended in time and space and be more or less integrated in a larger system of mutually reinforcing rules. An '*institution*' can be defined as a larger system of mutually reinforcing interconnected rules with a comparatively large extension in time and space, while '*institutionalization*' can be defined as the process through which such a rule system is developed and expanded in time and space.

What makes social actors follow rules? A distinction between *regulative, normative and cognitive mechanisms* (Scott 1995) seems useful in order to understand our rule-driven behaviour. '*Regulative mechanisms*' work through the stick and the carrot. Actors are assumed to follow a 'logic of consequentiality' (March & Olsen 1989). Within a 'logic of consequentiality', actors are assumed to calculate the consequences of different acts for their interests/goals. Regulative whip and carrot mechanisms work because they change the relative weight of advantages and disadvantages of the possible acts in a given situation.

The actor-structure perspective presented here is based on an interpretation of a sociological version of the new institutionalism in organizational analyses. From such a perspective, regulative mechanisms are considered less important than (or perhaps rather meaningless without) normative and cognitive mechanisms. Rules are rather/more often activated through a 'logic of appropriateness' (March & Olsen 1989; 1995) consisting of normative (what ought to be) as well as cognitive (what is) aspects.

Normative mechanisms have internal as well as external dimensions. In the internal dimension, social actors follow rules because they have internalized the norma-

Actors, Structures, and Rules 91

tive justifications of the rules ('democracy', 'justice', 'efficiency') as their own. Social actors follow rules because they consider them to be just, fair, efficient or the like, and thus think that they ought to follow them. In the external or relational dimension, human actors follow rules because they need to be able to justify their actions in relation to a prevailing public set of norms. Social actors might have internalized these norm systems to varying degrees, but they must at least be able to understand these norms and justify their actions appropriately.

Cognitive mechanisms consider the way we frame and perceive the world on a micro as well as on a macro level. Cognitive mechanisms are applied to the way we perceive 'the situation' and our role in it. In everyday life, we change rule systems or 'scripts' (Barley 1986) while we move from one setting to another or within the same setting without much consideration. Within a few minutes or even seconds, one set of rules replaces another by means of certain signals (what Goffman [1974] calls 'keying'). At the macro-level, an overall understanding of the situation is structurated by larger meaning systems, which means relatively coherent perceptions of how the world is and ought to be. For instance, the post-Second World War generation grew up with the Cold War and the notion of the First, Second and Third worlds. Future generations will need other concepts in order to make sense of the world. At the meso level, managers develop perceptions of the organizational field in which they work, and from such perceptions they elaborate a strategic understanding of the external threats and opportunities, and internal strengths and weaknesses of their organization. These frames of understanding structure the questions they ask and the answers they seek, as well as how problems are defined and possible solutions found.

What types of cultural rules are crucial for an understanding of managerial behaviour? Cultural rules exist on numerous levels, and I will argue that it is possible to work out a typology of rules that captures most of the structuration dynamics for people in managerial positions. As a first step, it may be useful to distinguish between a fourfold typology of rules based on affiliation, positions/relations, scenes and tasks which help structure managerial behavior. These four types of ruling systems must be understood within the larger social context of meaning and interaction that characterizes the specific organizational field, which in this case is the Danish municipal sector. Examples of the four ruling systems, and how they are activated by cognitive, normative and regulative mechanisms in the Danish municipal sector, are shown in table 7.1. *Rules of affiliation* concern such matters as hiring and firing managers and the career systems surrounding managerial positions. *Positional/relational rules* describe how players play roles and relate to each other as such. For example, in an inter-organizational context, one has the obligation to represent the organization. Another example is the set of formal or informal hierarchical relations between different organizations within an organizational field. In an intra-organizational context, hierarchical rules concerning authority ascribe relations between different players. *'Scene'-specific rules* are 'carried' by specific situations rather than specific actors, as demonstrated by Goffman (1959; 1974). Regarding the work of managers, the most obvious examples are the formal authority and detailed procedural rules ascribed to certain meetings. Finally, a number of the rules that structure managerial behaviour are *task-specific* – ie., connected to the task rather than to the actor or the scene.

Table 7.1: The structuration of managerial behaviour.

Mechanism \ Rules	*'Affiliation' rules*	*'Position' rules*	*'Scene' rules*	*'Task' rules*
Cognitive mechanisms Perceptions of reality (What is)	*Example:* Insecurity concerning one's affiliation to the organization has become a basic condition that is taken for granted.	*Example:* The rules concerning the interaction between the CEO and the mayor are taken for granted.	*Example:* The competence of the city council is taken for granted.	*Example:* The rules concerning municipal budgeting are taken for granted.
Normative mechanisms Evaluation of reality (What ought to be)	*Example:* Job insecurity has been internalized as a norm among many actors justified by arguments concerning more flexibility and incentives to make an extra effort.	*Example:* These rules are justified by democratic values internalized by most actors as just and fair.	*Example:* The competence of the city council is justified by democratic values internalized by most actors as just and fair.	*Example:* The rules of budgeting are justified by norms of democracy and rationality, and most actors have internalized these rules as their own.
Regulative mechanisms Rules are sanctioned by carrot-and-stick approaches	*Example:* Employment on a contractual basis has increasingly replaced the public servant status among managers in the public sector.	*Example:* Violation of the rules concerning the interaction with the mayor is punished by sanctions.	*Example:* Violation of the rules concerning the competence of the city council is punished by sanctions.	*Example:* Violation of the restrictions provided by the budget is punished by sanctions.

How are the four types of rule systems related to each other? Through education and career systems, 'affiliation' rules ensure that only individuals with an acceptable socially constructed 'habitus' (Bourdieu 1998) are allowed to enter 'the game'. Within the organization, 'affiliation rules' have an impact on the basic security of the job and ensure that certain types of behaviour enhance the chances of a brilliant career while other types of behaviour tend to spoil it. Since the right to hire and fire is usually ascribed to certain positions or scenes within an organization, 'affiliation' rules imply an asymmetric power relation between positions and scenes and often have a tacit, but important, impact on the daily interaction within the organization. 'Task' rules imply rules concerning who and how to handle specific tasks. Games on 'higher' levels in a hierarchy define opportunities, constraints and other rules on the 'lower' levels. This hierarchical dimension of social interaction (Mouzelis 1995) becomes obvious when analysing 'task' rules. 'Position' rules are related to 'task' rules in the sense that certain tasks are ascribed to certain positions, etc. While one feature of the managerial position is the power to change the division of labour within the organization, the four rule systems are interdependent and constitute a configuration of social relations, a management structure. It is through these conceptual lenses that the everyday life of Danish municipal CEOs will be analyzed. First, some contextual understanding of the position as a Danish CEO is required.

The Historical and Organizational Context

The municipalities in Denmark constitute the largest organizational field in the country. They employ more than 16% of the total workforce (equivalent to 482,679 full time positions) and spend more than 33% of the gross national product. Municipalities are responsible for primary schools, day-care institutions, all programs for the elderly (such as home-help, residential homes, old age pensions and various other forms of economic support), welfare payments, libraries, cultural activities, water supply, public parks, roads, refuse collection and environmental protection, to mention the more important tasks. All these tasks and programs are provided by an organization formally directed by the city council and supported by a professional municipal administration.

Not all the tasks carried out by municipalities at present have historically been handled by them. A major reform in 1970 changed the local governmental system in Denmark. Amalgamations took place, reducing the number of municipalities from around 1300 to 275. Many tasks were decentralized from the central government to the municipalities, and a common political and administrative structure for the municipalities was set up. The new structure prepared the ground for the large and professional municipal political-administrative management system in which the individual CEO is situated.

The relative autonomy of the municipalities is situated in a complex interaction with the central government, and a number of hierarchical rules are subject to constant negotiation and change. The basic task structure of the municipalities was decided by the central government in the 1970s. Since then, adaptive changes have been made, suggesting that a complex game concerning the adequate division of labour continues. This game concerns both the role and size of the Danish public sector and the division of labour within the public sector. Generally speaking, the individual municipality may decide the service level (spending, quality, coverage, etc.) on a large number of the services which are important to the welfare state. Municipal autonomy is relatively extensive as concerns the services produced by municipal institutions and more restricted with respect to income tranfers. Autonomy is further emphasized by the rights of local governments to fix their own tax rates. The income tax covers about half of municipal spending, the rest being covered by grants from the central government and fees and user charges (Jørgensen & Mouritzen 1993). Most of these 'rules of the game' cannot be changed by any individual CEO, but collectively, the associations of municipal managers participate in the constant reframing of the rules of the game at the national level.

Weaving the Social Bond as a Municipal CEO

The 'Affiliation' Rules

Rules of 'affiliation' have their own history. Some recent changes in the 'affiliation' rules of the Danish CEOs will be analyzed below, by focusing on the interaction between managerial behavior and career-patterns.

In Denmark, the CEO position has evolved from the former position of *town treasurer or town clerk*. The town clerk was the leading appointed official in most municipalities. However, the position was less influential than the present CEO position. The town clerk was in charge of the financial department and the secretariat of the town council. The typical town clerk began as a trainee in the municipal organization around the age of seventeen, followed by periods as assistant and municipal bookkeeper, finally becoming town clerk, typically within the same locality. In the large cities, the leading appointed official would in some cases have a university degree, typically in law. This was the situation in 1970 at the time of the municipal reform, and this tradition prevailed in 1980, at the time when a research project in the municipalities was being conducted (Riiskjær 1982; Flohr Nielsen 1985). In 1995, however, when the U.Di.T.E. project was conducted, major changes could be observed. These changes can be summarized in the following dimensions (Ejersbo *et al.* 1998):

- A change from internal recruitment to recruitment of people with an academic background. Among CEOs hired after 1989, 56% had academic backgrounds.
- An increasing turnover. Seventy-one percent of the CEOs have acquired their position within the last ten years. This contrasts with the situation in the early 1980s, when the CEO position implied life-long secure employment in the public sector. Among the resignations from 1990 to 1995 more than 33% were attributed problems of cooperation with politicians and approximately 25% to conflicts with fellow bureaucrats.
- It has become easier to fire municipal CEOs. Until a few years ago the CEOs (and the department heads as well) were appointed as civil servants with more or less life-long tenure due to the fiscal burden imposed upon the municipality by pre-retirement termination of employment. Today, an increasing number of CEOs are hired on contract for a fixed period, typically for six years, where the greater job insecurity is compensated by a higher annual salary.
- New demands on the CEOs. In the comparative analysis of job announcements for CEOs in the 1970s, 1980s and 1990s (Dahler-Larsen 1997), in the ideas concerning the roles of administrative managers formulated by the government in the 1980s (Bentzon 1988), and in other aspects (Hansen 1998), we find indications of the new demands imposed upon administrative municipal leaders. In the 1980s, functions as 'being in charge of the administration', 'secretary for the political body', and 'coordinating branches of administration' were significant. In the 1990s especially significant were 'to be advisor to the mayor' and to 'develop

services in the municipality'. Furthermore, we can observe a marked change in the personal attributes required from the CEOs. Today the CEO has to be visionary, to possess communication skills, to be able to motivate, have a sense of humour, etc.

The ability to manage the implementation of organizational change projects has been one of the new demands made on CEOs, and the following municipal tale explores some of the dynamics between career systems, success criteria and the manager's involvement in organizational change projects.

One of the small municipalities in Denmark was the first public organization to implement 'ethical accounting.'[1] Both the municipality and its leaders gained a reputation as modern and progressive. By the end of the 1980s, the reputation of being able to implement organizational change became a positive career parameter in the Danish municipal sector. The CEO from this municipality toured the country and explained the principles of ethical accounting. He complained that some municipalities misused the label, having applied only a small part of the concept. During our study, we found that even his own municipality had not applied the entire concept as he had described it in his speeches, although his municipality had plans to do so. This shortcoming was not at all a secret, but when listening to his speeches one had the impression that the ideas were implemented in the municipality. He simply did not make a clear distinction between present and future in these speeches. One year later, he was offered the job as municipal CEO in a larger municipality in Denmark, an offer which he accepted.

The idea of an 'ethical account' was 'sold' by the CEOs before it was fully implemented. Analytically, we can understand this by referring to phenomena such as organizational and managerial success criteria and image management and managerial career patterns. The municipality gains a reputation of being a progressive and successful organization. The CEO gains a reputation as a modern process- and change-oriented leader. This reputation gives him the opportunity to advance his career. This is not to say that the whole process is driven by rational calculations of the benefits and costs for the organization and the CEO. Rather, the CEO believes in these processes, and he finds challenges and pleasure in giving speeches. His mission is not to present a totally correct picture of reality in his municipality, but to inspire organizational change. He is not a scientist but an entrepreneur. The picture he presents is an interpretation of an ongoing process translated in a way which seeks to inspire an audience.

If the import of new ways of organizing becomes an important strategy for improving career opportunities as well as the successful reputation of the organization, it might have several consequences for the process of adaptation within the organi-

---

[1] In principle 'ethical accounting' implies a participative stakeholder approach (Bordum 1997). In a communicative process, important stakeholders agree upon a set of basic values. It is then regularly measured, usually by asking the same stakeholders whether the organization has complied with these values.

zation. The manager might leave the organization before the reform is adequately implemented, leaving the difficulties of implementation to others. This is not unusual in the Danish municipal context. More importantly, the manager might be more interested in the successful reputation of the reform than in its actual implementation (Baier, March & Sætren 1986). Managers might even hide or downplay the importance of implementation problems for such reasons. Often, however, they are simply not aware of the problems, since they have moved on in their career.

The Configuration of Positional/Relational and Scene-Specific Rules

The basic features of the Danish municipal political-administrative management structure were created in the 1970s. This structure consists of 'position' and 'scene' rules and rules concerning the relations between them, as illustrated in figure 7.1.

Figure 7.1: The municipal political-administrative management structure.*

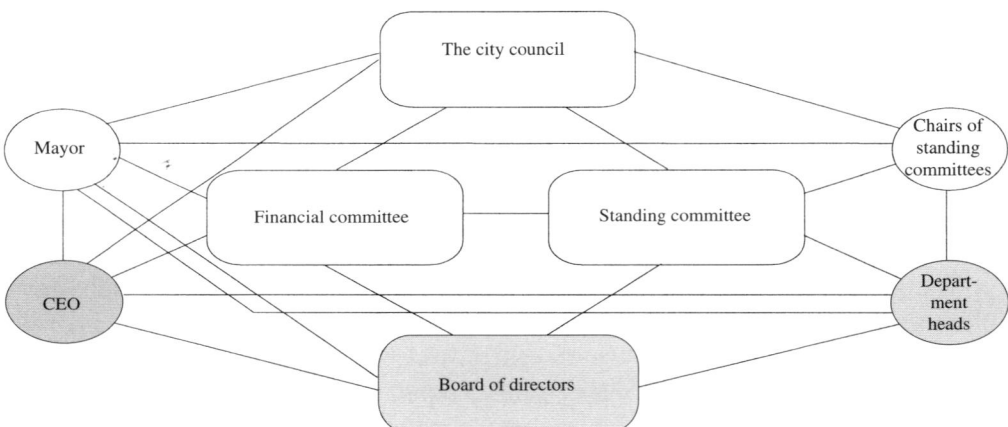

* The figure presents the basis structure in 270 of the Danish municipalities since the 1970s. The circles symbolize positions, while the rectangles symbolize scenes or decision-making areas. The white areas at the top constitute the political system, while the grey areas at the bottom constitute the administrative system. The number of standing committees, chairs of standing committees and department heads varies considerably between municipalities. There is only one city council, financial committee, mayor, CEO, and board of directors in each municipality.

When the task is to analyze the structuration of the CEO's work, an analysis of this configuration of position and scene specific relations is absolutely essential. The role and tasks of the CEO are, to a large extent, defined within this structure.

Formally speaking, the CEO is hired and can be fired by the city council. At meetings of the city council, the CEO plays the part of the loyal civil servant. He listens to the discussion, and answers questions from the politicians, but he never participates in the debate, except if asked to provide information or (rarely) to give his personal opinion. These scene-specific rules symbolically integrate the politicians and administrators in the parliamentary chain of command (Olsen 1978), which is normatively justified by democratic values, formally constituted in the law. Any violation of the rules will be followed by regulative mechanisms. The mayor is head of the city council and the financial committee. He or she is the only full-time employed elected politician in the municipal administration. All the tasks and responsibilities carried out by the CEO are by law assigned to the mayor. From a formal legal point of view, the CEO derives his authority from the mayor, and the mayor's authority derives from the city council and the financial committee. In reality, the city council and the financial committee are overloaded by the complexity of their tasks, and most mayors delegate substantial authority to the CEOs and employees in other parts of the administrative management structure. From the point of view of the CEO, two potential conflicts are inherent in the municipal management structure.[2] They are illustrated by the horisontally and vertically punctuated lines in figure 7.2.

One potential line of conflict represented by the horizontal line goes between the political and the administrative part of the structure. Another line of conflict represented by the vertical line goes between those responsible for specific parts of the municipal organization and those responsible for the whole of the organization. Both lines of conflict are well-known from empirical and theoretical literature concerning political-administrative management structures (Guy Peters 1995; Wildawsky 1974) and their implications will not be further elaborated here. The important point is that whatever the CEO does, and however (s)he decides to handle the role, the CEO will always have to face the potential conflicts inherent in the management structure. These conflicts will often produce dilemmas that can be managed but never solved. By improving their sense of the fine nuances of 'the game' and their abilities to communicate this understanding in management processes, CEOs might contribute considerably to improving (or worsening) the level of trust and cooperation within the structure. This achievement, however, will tend to be fragile and temporary within such a structure and must be constantly re-affirmed and re-created.

The Task-Specific Rules
Task-specific rules have certain basic features: (a) Historically, 'task' rules have been subject to political struggle within the welfare state. (b) The hierarchical dimension is very important, since the overall division of labour as well as a number of rules concerning how to fulfil the tasks are decided at the national level and to an increas-

---

[2] Conflicts may be rooted in cognitive, normative as well as regulative mechanisms. The assumption is that different positions in the structure will tend to evolve different perceptions of reality (cognitive mechanisms), be held accountable to different norms of appropriateness (normative mechanisms), and will be confronted with different sanctions (regulative mechanisms). Thus, conflicts may be rooted in a combination of one or more of these mechanisms.

Figure 7.2: Conflicts inherent in the municipal political-administrative management structure.*

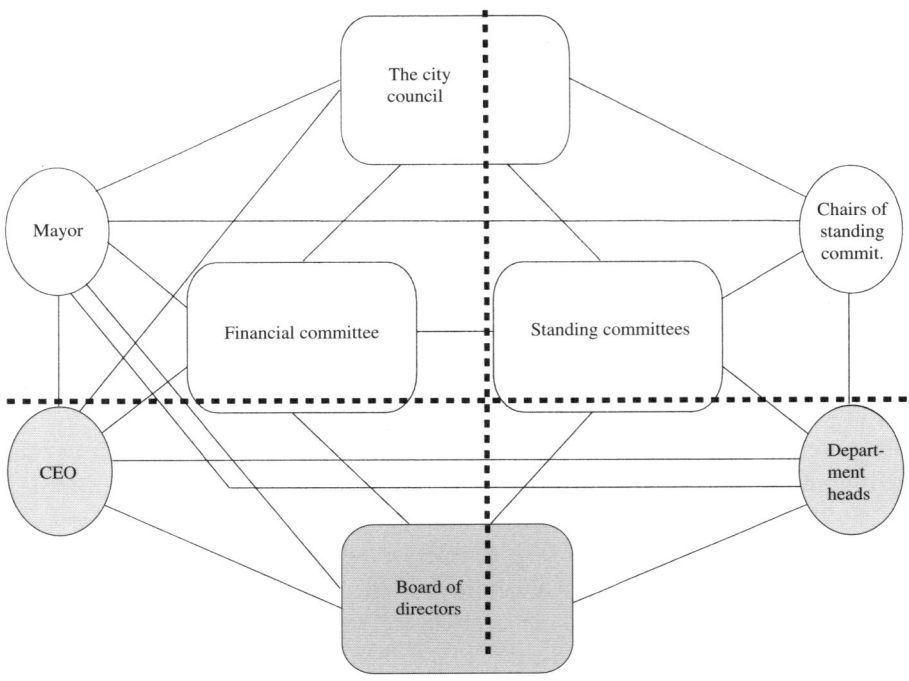

* The figure presents the basis structure in 270 of the Danish municipalities since the 1970s. The circles symbolize positions, while the rectangles symbolize scenes or decision-making areas. The white areas at the top constitute the political system, while the grey areas at the bottom constitute the administrative system. The number of standing committees, chairs of standing committees and department heads varies considerably between municipalities. There is only one city council, financial committee, mayor, CEO, and board of directors in each municipality.

ing extent even on the international (EU) level. (c) Within these constraints, the CEO has the authority to change at least some of the 'task' rules.

CEOs work on many different tasks and are able to define and prioritize their tasks to a larger extent than most other municipal actors. In most of their work, they also influence the priorities of other actors, although not necessarily in a deliberate way. CEOs invest a considerable amount of their time in the process of budgeting. Such a process involves all the positions and scenes in the municipal management structure. Some rules of budgeting are given hierarchically by the law. Other rules are given as rough guidelines due to a 'voluntary' agreement between the Ministry of Finance and the National Association of Local Authorities in Denmark. Other rules are given indirectly hierarchically by the obligations associated with specific municipal tasks. Generally speaking, the room for choice in the Danish municipalities will probably diminish in the next few years due to an expected higher increase in costs than in incomes. However, at least when it comes to procedural rules concerning how to organize the process of budgeting, there still seems to be plenty of room for experimentation within each municipality. And when it comes to the implementation of such a new process, the CEO often plays an important part. The organization of the process influences the distribution of power between positions and scenes within the municipal management structure. In the 1970s, for instance, the process of budgeting started in the standing committees in most municipalitites. This gave 'sector advocates' an important initiative in the process and enhanced the pressure towards increasing costs. Part of the strategy for increasing the economic steering capacity of the municipal management structure was to reorganize the process. In order to enhance the power of the guardians (Wildawsky 1974) the process of budgeting was in most municipalities reorganized in the 1980s so that the process started in the financial committees (Hansen 1998). This change probably increased the relative impact of the financial committee, the mayor and the CEO (the guardians) on the final budget.

Conclusion: the Institutional Embeddedness of Managerial Behaviour

The foregoing analysis of the institutional embeddedness of managerial behaviour provides a basic understanding of the tactical and strategical opportunities in a given situation.

The institutional perspective raises a number of important issues and questions for comparative cross-national research on the position of CEO. The first and perhaps most crucial issue is the role of the state in general and of the municipalities in particular, both in a functional and a symbolic sense. Even a superficial comparison of the history of Denmark and Portugal indicates that the significance ascribed to the state in the two societies varies considerably. In Denmark, the early 1970s were characterized by a great expansion of the municipalities, reform in their size and expansion of the tasks assigned to them. During this period, Portugal was involved in a colonial war in Africa and a struggle towards democracy at home. Although entities such as 'states' and 'municipalities' share some similarities, it is crucial to keep in mind that their functions, meanings and 'cultural rules' vary considerably in time and space.

Danish municipalities play a much more expanded role than municipalities in Portugal. *The differences in their function and degree of autonomy help explain the differences in the roles and range of choices available to Danish and Portuguese CEOs.*

In part, these differences reflect different rule-systems at the meso-level. Concerning the *rules of affiliation*, it makes a difference to what extent a national career system has evolved. Are CEOs primarily bounded in the local context, or are they part of a national corps of professional administrators? And how are the *configura-*

tion of rules about positions and scenes constructed? Although the formal rules are easier to compare, the informal rules may be more important. In the Danish case for instance, a number of detailed rules concerning the political part of the managerial configuration are constituted by law, while the administrative part is not even mentioned in the law. It is difficult to understand the managerial games in the Danish municipalities without some knowledge of the informal rules. A cross-national comparison of the formal rules could provide a good start for the analysis. Finally, the similarities and differences of *task rules* may be compared on a number of dimensions and analytical levels. The tasks assigned to the municipalities – and how these are organized within the municipal managerial configuration – tell us much about the potential role of the CEO. Such comparisons help us understand the different social bonds which affect and are determined by municipal CEOs.

CHAPTER 8

Threats and Challenges in the Organizational Environment Affecting the CEO

BY ANDY ASQUITH

Introduction

This chapter identifies a number of factors within the operating environment of local government chief executive officers (CEOs). Further, this chapter seeks to analyse the impact of these factors on the performance of the CEO. The factors are taken from the survey questionnaire used in the U.Di.T.E. Leadership Study. The U.Di.T.E. Leadership Study identified 12 factors which CEOs perceived to have a major impact on their performance, factors initially developed as a result of a pilot study conducted in Denmark. CEOs were asked to note their responses to questions asking what impact the factors had had on their role, on a 5 point scale – 'very high extent', 'high extent', 'some extent', 'little extent' and 'not at all'. For the purposes of analysis, it was felt necessary to consolidate these 12 factors into three themes. Table 8.1 below illustrates these thematic groupings.

Table 8.1: Thematic grouping of factors.

Theme 1: Finance and constitutionally related issues	*Theme 2:* Internal managerial and political issues	*Theme 3:* External citizen and community-related issues
• Financial problems in the municipality • Cuts in grants from upper-level governments • New regulations from upper-level governments • Central and/or regional government control of local government finances	• Lack of clear political goals • Conflicts between the political parties • Conflicts between the various departments and/or department heads • Unclear division of labour between politicians and the administration	• Demands of the population for better service • Demographic changes • Pressure from local organized interests, business and the like • Unemployment and social problems

In the analysis of the data, only those factors which CEOs perceived as having either a marked or unusual impact on their ability to fulfil their functions will be utilised in this chapter. This analysis will be conducted on two levels. First, where there is evidence within the thematic groupings that factors 'significantly correlate', these will be analysed. For the purpose of analysis, 'significant correlation' was deemed to be 0.400 or above. Every factor positively correlated with the other factors within each individual thematic group. The second level of analysis will focus on individual thematic factors, assessing differences among individual countries. However, before any of these factors can be examined for their impact upon the roles of local authority CEOs, it is essential that the changing roles of both local government and the CEO are placed in context.

Setting the Scene

It is generally agreed that since the oil crisis and subsequent world wide economic recession of the mid 1970s, local government in the western hemisphere (and indeed public sectors as a whole) have been undergoing profound change (Eliassen & Kooiman 1993; Ferlie *et al.*1996; Flynn & Strehl 1996; Hughes 1994; Isaac-Henry 1997). Indeed, evidence abounds of radical public sector change programmes in Australia (Castles *et al.* 1996; Watt 1997), Ireland (Asquith & O'Halpin 1996a; 1998; Boyle *et al.* 1997), New Zealand (Castles *et al.* 1996; Gosling 1997), and the United States of America (Nichols Clark 1994; Osborne & Gaebler 1992; Svara 1996). Bennis *et al.* (1976) and Waterman (1988), though not referring to the public sector, nevertheless appear to offer an accurate description of the state of public sector management in their observation that the 'only constant is change'. Quirk (1991), writing as a senior English local government officer, argued that 'transformation' rather than 'change' is the appropriate term to apply to the state of local government, given the extent and impact of local government change agendas. Observers thus seem to agree that there has been a fundamental reappraisal of the nature and role of local authorities, and of public sectors as a whole.

Traditional values, structures and practices of local authorities have been challenged by management models whose philosophical bases rest firmly within the private business sector (Hood 1991; Pollitt 1993). Public administration has to some extent been replaced by public management. Traditional bureaucratic and administrative structures and organisations (cf. Alexander 1982; Headrick 1962) are perceived to be no longer valid in today's rapidly changing consumer society (Keenan 1993). The Weberian mode of running public sector organisations was viewed as outdated. Whereas public sector organisations were once viewed as static institutions which did not change, and which administered services characterised by continuity, public services now clearly exist in a volatile environment, and are subject to the increasingly whimsical preferences of both elected politicians and service users. As such, services can now be said to be customer- or client-led rather than provider led

(Osborne & Gaebler 1992). Commenting on this rise of 'new public management' (Hood 1991) or 'managerialism' (Pollitt 1993) thinking, Hughes observes that:

> Recent changes to the public sector have led to fundamental questioning of its role and place in society. The main point to be made here is that a new paradigm governing the management of the public sector has emerged, one that moves the public sector inexorably away from administration towards management. It needs to be emphasised that government and a public service are vital to economic success and to social cohesion. The decade of the 1980s saw major changes in the management and scope of the public sector. Instead of dismantling the government, we are witnessing now the beginning of a new form of government and governance [1994, 21-2].

Flynn (1997) and Johnson (1997) accredit much of this change to the rise of the ideas of the so-called 'New Right', who gave intellectual rigour to the aspirations of, principally, the governments of Hawke and Keating (in Australia); Lange, Palmer and Moore (in New Zealand); Reagan and Bush in the United States) and Thatcher and Major (in the United Kingdom). The New Right, supported by public choice theorists such as Niskanen (1971, 1973), gained prominence in political and academic circles in the mid-1970s, with their 'solution' to the problems created by the world wide recession. The public choice theorists argued that government, particularly those associated with Keynesian economic policies, stifled individual choice and freedom, and that less government was needed to stimulate depressed economies and simultaneously enhance individual freedom. Income paid out in taxation was income which the rational, utility maximising individual was unable to choose how to spend (cf. Jordan & Ashford 1993; McLean 1987). As such, the agenda of the 'New Right' contained four principal planks: (1) the curtailment of growth in public expenditures; (2) a belief in the workings of the free market; (3) enhancement of individual choice and development of 'self-reliance'; and (4) the ending of what was seen as the 'nanny state', meaning the targeting of resources to those groups in society deemed to be in genuine need of the welfare state's expenditure (Barry 1991; Self 1993).

Central to the theoretical and philosophical underpinnings of the New Right's stance is the argument that the post-war social democratic consensus which had dominated politics in the western hemisphere since 1945 was no longer valid. The post-war consensus had advocated a mixed economy with a substantial welfare state, a situation perceived in some quarters to be unsustainable because of the costs involved (Niskanen 1971; 1973; Stigler 1975). Hence, the political supporters of the New Right have argued for a much smaller public sector with an increased role in service provision for the private and voluntary sectors, to be achieved through competition on grounds of cost (Barry 1991; Jordan & Ashford 1993; Ridley 1988). Despite the very clear linkages that exist between public choice theorists and 'conservative' politicians on the right of the political spectrum, it is nevertheless important to note that support for public choice theory, and its implicit implications, also exists among politicians of the 'left', and indeed common across the political spectrum is the emphasis on 'value for money,' a concept central to the dogma of managerialism (Kerley 1994; Rouse 1997).

The radical change agendas which were embarked upon by Labour Governments in both Australia and New Zealand (cf. Gosling 1997; Castles *et al.* 1996; Watt 1997) and by Clinton's Democratic administration in the United States (cf. Osborne & Gaebler 1992) owe much to public choice theory, as does the evolving political agenda of the Blair Labour Government in the United Kingdom (Hutton 1995; 1997a; 1997b). However, the differentiating factor between governments of the right and of the centre/left is that whilst the former adopt a stance which is distinctly anti-government, the latter view government as a necessary feature of civilised society; rather than abandoning government, the centre/left simply wishes to re-invent it in order to enhance both its effectiveness and its perceived relevance to the lives of citizens (Painter 1994; Peters 1997).

The changes affecting local government, can, according to Asquith (1997) and Morris and Paine (1995), come from 'external' or 'internal' forces. By 'external' is meant primarily the action of central government through legislation, whereas and 'internal' or local forces denote the actions taken by individual authorities themselves, either proactively or in response to the desires or requirements of individuals or groups of citizens amongst the publics they are elected to serve. The real extent of externally driven change can be seen in the fact that in the UK between 1979 and 1997, 210 Acts of Parliament were directly concerned with the activities of local authorities (Wilson & Game 1998). Such an active legislative agenda led Davis (1988) to suggest that local government was in effect 'under siege', while Wilson and Game (1998) observe that the ability of local authorities to comprehend and accommodate wave after wave of change represents a fundamental cultural shift for them. Indeed, the ability of local authorities to handle such a concerted period of intense change, all the while retaining their respective corporate identities, speaks volumes for the managerial and leadership skills demonstrated by the CEOs.

Theme 1: Finance and Constitutionally-Related Issues

The U.Di.T.E. Leadership Study sought the views of CEOs on four questions related to financial and constitutional issues. Specifically, the questions sought to ascertain the extent to which these issues have impacted upon the CEOs' ability to perform their role in recent years. These issues are identified in table 8.2.

Table 8.2: Finance and constitutionally-related issues.

- Financial problems in the municipality
- Cuts in grants from upper-level governments
- New regulations from upper-level governments
- Central and/or regional government control of local government finances

Within this thematic group, it was somewhat surprising to find that there were only two correlations in excess of 0.400 – those relating to financial problems/ cuts in grants from upper-level government and upper level control of local finances/ cuts in grants from upper-level government. This is illustrated in table 8.3 below.

Table 8.3: Correlation of finance and constitutionally-related issues (N = 4226).

Factors	New regulations	Control of local finances	Cuts in grants
Financial problems	0.232	0.335	0.452
New regulations		0.365	0.322
Control of local finances			0.421

Of the three thematic groups, those concerned with finance and constitutionally-related issues show the highest levels of positive correlation. This is hardly surprising, given the fact that in all organisations, not just local authorities, finance is the engine which drives the organisation forward. Added to this is the fact that many local authorities must exist with powerful national governments. Hence, had the data analysis not produced such a picture, there would have been a high degree of incredulity. However, this significant dependent relationship indicated only those correlations relating to financial problems/cuts in grants from upper-level government and upper level control of local finances/cuts in grants from upper-level government. Hence, it is clear that the financial problems and level of national government support are indeed inter-related.

This probably illustrates a country effect: as some national governments seem to be increasingly centralising those features of policy making which may impact upon macro-economic aims and objectives, the result is a decline in local financial autonomy/independence of local elected sub-national authorities.

Given the seemingly perpetual need to limit public expenditure and achieve 'value for money' (Kerley 1994; Rouse 1997), it is perhaps surprising to find the wide deviations in responses from different countries on these important issues. Indeed, despite what has been portrayed as an international crusade by respective national governments to achieve the 'holy grail' of VFM (cf. Hughes 1994), these differences in response are most interesting. Despite this general picture though, there is a noticeable deviation in the individual country figures for the Netherlands, Belgium and Portugal in relation to financial problems/cuts in grants from upper-level government. Similarly, there are noticeable deviations in individual country figures from Sweden and the Netherlands in relation to upper level control of local finances/cuts in grants from upper-level government. These are analysed below.

In terms of financial problems/cuts in grants from upper-level government, a two-dimensional view can be seen from table 8.4.

Table 8.4: Extent to which financial problems/cuts in grants have a 'high'/'very high' impact upon CEOs' role.

	Country			Average
Factor	The Netherlands	Belgium	Portugal	All countries
Financial problems	10.7%	13.5%	12.0%	26.1%
Cuts in grants	6.4%	16.5%	7.5%	31.8%

This illustrates the levels to which CEOs were influenced to a 'high'/'very high' extent by the actions of upper level governments and general finance related problems in these three countries against the average of all participating countries. The statistical data would appear to indicate that within these three countries, national governments have the least negative impact upon the autonomy of the CEOs.

In terms of the correlation between the figures for upper level control of local finances/cuts in grants from upper-level government, it is useful to use a two-dimensional illustration to demonstrate an unusual result. This is shown in table 8.5.

Table 8.5: Extent to which control of local finances/cuts in grants have a 'high'/'very high' impact upon CEOs' role.

	Country		
Factor	Sweden	The Netherlands	Average
Control of local finances	15.4%	2.2%	29.5%
Cuts in grants	64.6%	6.4%	31.8%

The figures for Sweden and the Netherlands are again shown against the average of all participating countries in order to illustrate the impact of upper level government control of local finance. Table 8.5 shows the extent to which CEOs in both Sweden and the Netherlands felt that to a 'high'/'very high' extent, the issue of upper-level governments seeking control of local finances had *not* impacted upon their roles. These figures must be seen against a cross-national average which is much higher. One can conclude from this that in these two countries, national governments have shown less of a propensity to reduce local financial autonomy. What is also of interest from table 8.5 is the substantial difference between the two countries and the issue of central government attempts to cut grants to local authorities. This difference is surprising given the relatively high level of correlation between the two factors identified in table 8.5. Clearly within Sweden, the national government while not seeking to control local authority spending, is nevertheless seeking to exercise its influence through substantial reductions in grants paid out to local government. In pursuing such a policy, the Swedish Government is not necessarily driven by a desire to 'control' local government expenditure; rather, it seeks to end the severe economic recession endured by Sweden.

The figures for two other countries warrant further note and comment. We have already mentioned the productivity rate of the United Kingdom central government as concerns legislation affecting local authorities between 1979-1997. As much of this legislation was related to attempts to stem local government expenditure, it is perhaps unsurprising to find that some 70% of United Kingdom CEOs felt either 'highly' or 'very highly' that central government financial controls had had a negative impact on their ability to carry out their tasks. A similar response level was found in Ireland, where the democratic component of local government is very weak (Roche 1982). This inherent electoral/democratic weakness in Irish local government effectively means that actors concerned with local government have very little legitimacy upon which to base their arguments when intervention and change originate with central government. This point concerning legitimacy is further demonstrated in Ireland, where the ability of local authorities to raise taxes is severely limited. Over 50% of CEOs stated that generally, financial difficulties impeded upon their role either 'highly' or 'very highly'. One of the distinguishing features of local *government*, as opposed to local *administration*, that of the power to tax, has been fundamentally weakened in Ireland.

As alluded to above, the 'flip side' of this potentially depressing view can quite clearly be found in both Belgium and the Netherlands, where 80% of CEOs responded that the financial control exerted by central government had either 'very little' or 'no' negative impact on their roles. In addition, support for this Dutch position exists in the fact that not a single Dutch CEO felt that central government financial control had a 'very high' impact on his/her role. Further to this point, the Netherlands, where less than 3% of CEOs felt constrained by financial control, would appear to be best place to be a local authority CEO if one desired a working environment in which local government was relatively free of financial restrictions!

Theme 2: Internal Managerial and Political Issues

The U.Di.T.E. Leadership Study sought the views of CEOs on four questions related to internal managerial and political issues. Specifically, the questions sought to ascertain the extent to which these issues have impacted upon the CEOs' ability to perform their role in recent years. These issues are identified in table 8.6.

Table 8.6: Internal managerial and political issues.

- Lack of clear political goals
- Conflicts between the political parties
- Conflicts between the various departments and/or department heads
- Unclear division of labour between politicians and the administration

Within this thematic group, it was again unexpected to find that there were only 2 correlations in excess of 0.400, those relating to lack of clear political goals/unclear division of labour, and conflicts between departments/unclear division of labour. This is illustrated in table 8.7 below.

Table 8.7: Correlation of internal managerial and political issues.

Factors	Political conflict	Departmental conflict	Unclear division of labour
Lack of political goals	0.330	0.272	0.482
Political conflict		0.257	0.365
Departmental conflict			0.404

It is worth noting at this juncture that two countries exhibited markedly different results from the other countries in the survey. Data from Italy and Spain appear to indicate a lack of internal organisational managerial unity and an unclear strategic management role for CEOs in these two countries. On the other hand, the data relating lack of political goals/unclear division of labour clearly reinforce the position of the powerful Irish local government manager. The data for Ireland on these two issues deviate markedly from the cross-national average.

Given that local authorities have had to deal, and indeed will increasingly have to deal, with a considerable amount of change, let us examine how the authorities intend to accommodate such change. Apart from accommodating the change, authorities also need to be able to effectively manage it, so as to ensure that the change has the desired effect, all the while maintaining the basic infrastructure of the welfare state for which they are responsible. Crucial in managing this change is the CEO's role and ability to manage both political and administrative relationships *within* the organisation. The importance of the CEO being able to competently manage *external* relationships is examined later in this chapter.

The increasingly turbulent environment within which local authorities exist has given rise to a 'new public management' (Hood 1991; Hughes 1994; Pollitt 1993). This has evolved because of the realisation within public sector organisations that traditional incremental (administrative) approaches to policy making and management were 'inefficient and wasteful' and therefore detrimental to a 'cost effective' delivery of public services (Asquith 1997; Asquith & O'Halpin 1996a; 1998; Painter 1997; Alexander 1982; Elcock 1994; Headrick 1962). Public service management has been specifically concerned with the change *management* processes now required in the public sector, all the while stressing concepts such as 'strategic management', 'vision' and 'leadership' more familiarly associated with the private business sector (cf. Hesselbein *et al.* 1997a; 1997b).

The rise of the public sector manager, as opposed to the more traditional administrator or bureaucrat, has meant that internal roles within local authorities have had to be redefined. Whereas the CEO, or his/her equivalent within an essentially Weberian bureaucracy would have been *primus inter pares* such a relationship is no longer viable (Alexander 1982). In a number of countries, the designation of the CEO as the leader of the managerial side of the managerial/political interface within a local authority resulted in varying degrees of internal harmony and conflict. For example, Italian and Spanish local government CEOs were distinguished from their counterparts elsewhere by the fact that they felt that departmental conflict was twice as likely to have either a 'high'/'very high' impact upon their ability to carry out their functions than their counterparts elsewhere. This is shown in table 8.8.

Table 8.8: Extent to which departmental conflict and unclear division of labour have a 'high'/'very high' impact upon CEOs' role.

	Country		
Factor	Italy	Spain	Average
Departmental conflict	24.5%	19.7%	10.6%
Unclear division of labour	57.1%	49.0%	22.2%

Likewise, CEOs from Italy and Spain exhibited a much higher indication that an unclear division of labour had a 'high'/'very high' effect in their performance. Local authorities in both these countries seem to be somewhat uncertain and unstable in relation to the role of the CEOs, the position of fellow officers/managers and with elected politicians. Such uncertainty can only lead to the CEO being diverted from the overall strategy of the local authority, since more time must be spent dealing with the minutiae of internal conflict.

This shift in management thinking and practice is clearly demonstrated by a number of commentators (Asquith & O'Halpin 1996a; 1998; Morris & Paine 1995; Morphett 1993; Norton 1991; Painter 1997) who place considerable emphasis on the requirement of a CEO to develop and effectively communicate an appropriate organisational vision to the stakeholders of the authority. Indeed this point is made by one former senior English local authority chief executive officer, Sabin, who described his role as 'setting out the corporate cultural values, encompassing the organisational vision and style, so that the principles can take effect in practice' (1990, 26).

Although much has been written about this management of change process, the majority of this work has been principally concerned with the private sector (cf. Hesselbein *et al.* 1997a; 1997b; Kanter 1990; Morgan 1988; Peters 1992). However, a growing number of studies are focusing on the workings of the public sector (Ferlie *et al.* 1996; Flynn 1997; Hughes 1994; Isaac-Henry *et al.* 1997; Ranson & Stewart 1994). This work has concluded that transferring unmodified and generic private sector management techniques to the public sector would likely undermine the very traditions upon which the public sector was based. Ranson and Stewart comment on these differences:

> It is the principal purpose of the public domain to develop those institutions and values which enable citizens to flourish not only as individuals but also in their contribution to the life and well-being of society. The failure of the polity ... is to have abandoned this understanding of its purpose, not least because its own legitimacy and thus survival depends upon the authority it derives from public consent. The challenge for the public domain and its management is to rediscover the foundations of democratic citizenship that alone can regenerate the quality of life for the public as a whole [1994, xi].

Asquith (1994) and Flynn (1997) have assessed the scope for transferring private sector techniques to the public sector, seeking to suggest modifications that will ease the transfer. In seeking to modify traditional private sector management techniques, writers are acknowledging that the basis of the public sector differs fundamentally from the private sector (cf. Ranson & Stewart 1994). Whereas the private sector is founded upon the profit motive and wealth creation, the public sector is (normatively) under democratic control and is concerned with the concept and values of public service provision, as well as being subject to a higher degree of electoral accountability and legislative control than is to be found in traditional commercial enterprises.

Hence, emphasis on the political environment is the one specific factor which distinguishes public sector organisations from those within the private and voluntary sectors. There were, however, markedly differing degrees by which the 'political' nature of local authorities exhibited themselves in the CEO responses to the U.Di.T.E. Leadership Study questionnaire, specifically in relation to the relation between a lack of political goals and the extent to which party political conflict impacted upon the CEOs role. By far the most intriguing results to both these questions were from those countries with a tradition of local authority management as opposed to traditional bureaucratic administration under a nominal political leadership. In Ireland, Australia and the United States, over 80% of CEOs responded that in their authority there was 'little' or 'no' political conflict which could impinge upon their role. This is illustrated in table 8.9.

Table 8.9: Extent to which political authority has 'little'/'no' impact upon CEOs' role.

	Country			Average
Factor	Ireland	Australia	United States	All countries
Political conflict	80.2%	84.2%	87.9%	69.3%

In the case of Ireland, a series of Management Acts have enshrined into law clear and distinct powers to Irish CEOs at the expense of the locally legitimised Irish councillors (Collins 1987; O'Halpin 1991). Given this situation, it is hardly surprising that Irish CEOs feel untroubled by political conflict. In a similar vein, no Irish CEOs felt restricted to a 'high' or a 'very high extent' in their position by an absence of a political vision for their local authority, a reflection of their own recognised power and self-confidence (Asquith & O'Halpin 1996b; 1997). What is notable overall, however, is that in the other countries surveyed, where CEOs are ostensibly under the control of democratically elected local councillors, these CEOs do not feel so concerned! This can clearly be seen as a reflection of the power, and rightly so, of the ballot box in local government.

In order to grasp and fully utilise the opportunities offered by the techniques involved in the management of the change confronting them, local authorities must develop a strategy to not only successfully implement the change process, but one which will also enable them to become proactive, forward-looking organisations (Asquith 1997; Leach & Collinge 1998). Organisations which exist in turbulent environments, if they are to survive, must have a strategy that is flexible and responsive enough to meet rapidly changing environmental circumstances. For many local authorities, there are two prerequisites: the creation of a shared organisational culture and the establishment of both an organisational vision and mission. Both these tasks are clearly within the remit of the CEO, who must translate the political aspirations of the elected councillors into an achievable operational agenda.

Theme 3: External Citizen and Community Related Issues

The U.Di.T.E. Leadership Study sought the views of CEOs on four questions related to citizen and community-related issues. Specifically, the questions sought to ascertain the extent to which these external issues have impacted upon the CEOs ability to perform their role in recent years. These issues are identified in table 8.10.

Table 8.10: External citizen and community related issues.

- Demands of the population for better service
- Demographic changes
- Pressures from local organized interests, business and the like
- Unemployment and social problems

Within this thematic group, there were no correlations in excess of 0.400. This is illustrated in table 8.11. below.

Table 8.11: Correlations among citizen and community related issues.

Factors	*Demographic changes*	*Interest group pressure*	*Social issues*
Better service	0.352	0.294	0.331
Demographic changes		0.388	0.240
Interest group pressure			0.235

Given the economic and political background of the organisational agendas of many local authorities, the whole 'management of change' process may perhaps be described as the 'management of cultural change'. This is because the impact of the change effectively involves the creation of a whole new organisational culture, i.e. the shift from an administratively driven organisation to one with a distinctly managerialist outlook. This entails the creation of a shared set of core values, something which permeates the whole organisation, values which must enjoy common ownership not only amongst those employed within the organisation, but also by all those affected by the organisation's actions, its so-called 'stakeholders' (Newman 1994; 1996). The lack of significant correlations is therefore somewhat surprising given the international wave of reforms which emphasise the importance of the wider community in the development, delivery and assessment of public services. *The results may be indicative of the broad spectrum of influences and pressures within the local authority environment.* As such, it may simply not be possible to achieve the 'ideal' situation of community involvement in public service development, delivery and assessment advocated by some.

The term 'stakeholders' refers to individuals and or groups who may be affected by the actions of an organisation. In terms of a local authority, stakeholders include its elected members, the electorate, service users (and importantly, non-users), the voluntary and private sectors and the authority's employees. It is increasingly accepted that each stakeholder has a legitimate right to have an input into the planning and provision of local authority services. Indeed, within the United Kingdom, the recently elected Labour Government is embarking upon a major policy vis-à-vis local government which will enshrine into law the rights of such stakeholders. The policy, known as 'Best Value', seeks to ensure that stakeholders, especially those outside the local authority (as opposed to those 'within') are consulted on important aspects of service planning, delivery and importantly, evaluation (Bedford Borough Council 1997; Wilson & Game 1998).

Despite this alleged citizen pressure for better or increased levels of public service provision, evidence from the survey data does not appear to support this view. What is intriguing from the data analysed within the U.Di.T.E. Leadership Study is that in those countries with historically vibrant, strong systems of local politics and government, there appears to be little demand for better services (from citizens) which impacts adversely on the CEOs' role. Rather, it is those countries with a long-standing history of local authority management (Ireland, Australia and the United States) in which citizen pressure for better public services is most important. This is shown in table 8.12.

It could be argued that the major reason for this statistical picture is that the local authority CEOs in Ireland, Australia and the United States are in effect the first line of executive power within their respective organisations. The CEOs are the single or primary source of executive authority within their particular local government unit. Therefore, citizens clamouring for improvements in services do not see the need to lobby elected politicians who may be perceived as powerless. Rather, citizens seek

Table 8.12: Extent to which citizen demands have 'high'/'very high' impact upon CEOs' role.

	Country			Average
Factor	Ireland	Australia	United States	All countries
Demand for better service	19.9%	16.6%	22.5%	12.0%

the ear of the person they perceive to be the holder of executive power: the CEO.

A more general point is apparent about the role of overall pressure group activity in influencing the political decision-making processes within local authorities. Among all the countries participating in the research, 70% of CEOs reported that pressure groups have either 'little' or 'no' impact upon their roles as local authority managers. In addition, what is also surprising is the fact that pressure groups appear to have little overall impact, even in those local authorities which do not appear to have a clear political direction, and as such could be said to suffer from political drift. Such 'drifting' local authorities, it could be argued, would be ideal arenas in which pressure groups could most successfully exert their influence.

One other factor of note which emerges from the data analysis is the differing impacts of unemployment and social problems upon the CEOs' role. These differences are clearly illustrated by reference to the data relating to Finland and Belgium. This data is produced below in table 8.13 which also notes the levels of interest group pressure in these two countries.

Table 8.13: Extent to which social factors have a 'high'/'very high' impact upon CEOs' role.

	Country		
Factor	Finland	Belgium	Average
Social issues	47.0%	1.9%	16.4%
Interest group pressure	3.6%	3.8%	7.7%

Such stark differences in the perceived relative importance of unemployment and social problems may have two possible causes. Either Finnish local government, as opposed to, for example, Belgian local government, is charged with a clear statutory role in tackling such social issues as unemployment, or there is a perception among Finns that their local authorities can help alleviate some of the hardship associated with these problems. However, given the lack of organised pressure from local interest groups illustrated in table 8.13, assuming this as the most likely form of citizen mobilisation, the latter explanation seems implausible. What appears to be happening, therefore, is that unlike their counterparts elsewhere, Finnish CEOs and the organisations they lead are charged with considerable responsibility for tackling the general problem of unemployment and associated social problems at the expense of the role of central government.

These changes and developments in service provider/user relationships have fundamental consequences for the existing management systems and practices which have hitherto been commonplace within local government. The provision of services by public sector organisations has by convention been provided very much in a 'Fordist' style (Brooke 1991; Leach *et al.* 1994; Skelcher 1992). Formerly, there was no real grasp of concepts such as 'consumerism' and 'customer service'. Rather, as noted above, local authorities tended to be bureaucratic, producer led, dominated by local government professionals, paying scant attention to the aspirations and needs of the service user – or indeed the non-service user. As society has become more consumer-oriented, many local authorities have sought to reform their systems and practices so as to make the services they provide 'user-led' (Asquith & O'Halpin 1998; Painter 1997).

A local authority, if it is to survive in its ever-changing socio-economic and political environment, must develop a culture which can clearly recognise these changes and act accordingly. Of fundamental importance to the management of change in local government is to acknowledge that local authorities have become 'user'-led rather than 'producer'-led organisations, a change that Skelcher (1992) and Wilson and Game (1998) categorise as a shift from the provision of 'paternalistic' to 'excellent' services. Such a change has led to the realisation (Osborne & Gaebler 1992; Painter 1994) that the most important interface within any (service) organisation is that between service users or consumers and the 'street level' operatives who provide the actual service. Here, much of the work picks up on themes developed by Stewart and Clarke (1987) in their seminal article describing the 'public service orientation'.

Stewart and Clarke (1987) sought to prescribe not so much a model of local government, but rather a model of *local governance* which would reinvigorate all features of local democracy and specifically recognise the key role of street-level operatives. It is often the case that the first point of contact between a service user and a local authority will be the street level operative. Hence, the street level operator plays a key role in how a service user will perceive not only the local authority but also the services it provides. As such, the street-level operative plays an important role in what may be the initial linkage between local government and citizens. Such a realisation, that of the importance of street-level operatives, has a major 'knock-on' effect for the traditional internal systems (and structures) within local authorities. It is essential that systems previously based on both hierarchical and professional barriers and boundaries should now reflect the more consumer-oriented flexible approach to service development and delivery. In effect, what is required is the inverting of the hierarchical pyramid and the abolition of previously sacred professional boundaries. Burns and Stalker (1961) argue that it is essential to invert the hierarchical pyramid in times of environmental turbulence, because traditional bureaucratic management structures are incapable of coping with the 'alien' tasks such turbulence invariably creates.

Implications

The actions of local authorities seeking to implement organisational change agendas in order to accommodate their respective change programmes closely reflect the organisational change theory that views organisations as living organisms (Asquith 1997; Espejo 1989; Isaac-Henry & Painter 1991b; Morgan 1986). Since such organisms inhabit constantly changing environments, they will effectively 'die' should they cease to adapt. Local authorities have simply had to change to accommodate 'wave after wave' of change. To simply do nothing would have resulted in the loss of functions, the cumulative effect of which would have led to their eventual extinction. As Isaac-Henry and Painter state: 'Organisations under threat from the impact of rapid change can all too easily become introspective, defensive and even fatalistic about their future' (1991a, p.1).

While it could be argued that it is highly unlikely for a local authority, or indeed any public sector organisation to be allowed to 'die', the actions of certain national governments suggest otherwise. In recent years, in the United Kingdom (cf. Wilson & Game 1998) and the United States (cf. Osborne & Gaebler 1992) there is evidence that under-performing public sector organisations, or those perceived by national government to be under-performing, have been left to 'wither'. Such institutions have subsequently been replaced by organisations deemed by national governments to operate in a far more efficient manner.

It could be argued, however, that for a local authority to pursue such a minimalist strategy is in effect an abdication of its duties (cf. Asquith 1994; 1997; Wilson & Game 1998). Local authorities were created to enhance the social well-being of citizens through the exercise of political power in the local arena. The use of such legitimised power was designed to improve the quality of life for all an area's citizens. Rather than abdicate power, local authorities ought to be seeking to exercise the influence and power their democratic base uniquely gives them. While there is evidence that in some countries financial restrictions effectively limit the direct power of CEOs and local authorities to act (see above), it is possible to identify local authorities which have sought alternative ways of exercising their legitimacy. Stewart (1988) writes about the 'management of influence' rather than the use and management of direct (financial) power, while Osborne and Gaebler (1992), Peters (1997) and Ranson and Stewart (1994) all describe different ways in which (local) government can operate effectively in the name of governance.

Local authorities can thus be seen as evolutionary organisations which exist in a turbulent environment. As such, local authorities have had to reassess many of the ways they have previously performed their functions. Central to this has been the cultural reorientation which has taken place within many local authorities, reorientations which have had major repercussions for the systems, practices (and structures) of local authorities. Closely allied to this change within authorities' culture is the requirement that organisations which exist in constantly changing environments have some form of organisational strategy: a vision and a mission of what the organisation is seeking to become. This strategy will itself be guided by the principal organisational change agent and leader: the CEO. Certo and Peter draw the connection between all these points:

> The significance of organisational culture for implementing strategies is that it influences the behaviour of employees and, it is hoped, motivates them to achieve or surpass organisational objectives. Typically, the chief executive officer and other present or past leaders in an organisation are the key agents influencing the culture [1991, 141].

What is clear from the evidence in this chapter is that the role of local government, and with it, the role of the local government CEO is undergoing profound change. Equally evident is the fact while local authorities are adapting to accommodate change which is essentially imposed by national/central government, local authorities are also evolving organisations. In order to take advantage of the many opportunities afforded to them, and in order to continually provide effective services to their citizens, local authorities have undergone, and are indeed undergoing, organisational re-inventions. Key to these processes are the CEOs.

This chapter has used a number of examples to illustrate the pressures and influences exerted upon local government, pressures which can have a major impact upon the ability of the CEO to fulfil his/her role. Despite these pressures, the CEOs, through their ingenuity and initiative, have demonstrated their ability to steer their organisations through periods of immense uncertainty. Moreover, the CEOs have been able to re-invigorate their authorities, re-enforcing both the managerial and democratic dimensions of local governance. This, if nothing else, is an illustration of the inherent skills and abilities of the local authority CEO.

CHAPTER 9

Leaving the Job as CEO

BY NIELS EJERSBO AND PETER DAHLER-LARSEN

Introduction

De-recruitment takes place when a person leaves a job. Some may leave because of age. Thirty years ago, 60% of CEOs in Western local government who had left their jobs did so due to natural causes. Over the years this reason for derecruitment has decreased. In the last five years, natural causes account for one-third of the derecruitment, but continue to be the most important single factor.

Some CEOs quit their job because of the workload. This factor constitutes only a small portion of the total derecruitment, and it has not changed much over time. Others may be forced out of the organization due to problems of cooperation with politicians or bureaucrats. This accounts for about 20% of the total derecruitment of CEOs today, and the figure has been increasing over time.

A career plan leading to a more prestigious or better paid job can be an important reason for moving to another job. This factor also accounts for about 20% of the total derecruitment in the countries in our survey. Derecruitment has been increasing over time, except for an extraordinarily high frequency about 15-20 years ago, perhaps due to reforms in several countries.

For local government CEOs, job security is likely to be one of the key factors influencing the overall attractiveness of the job. An indication that job security has considerable value is found in cases of fixed-term contracts which are used to an increasing extent in Denmark. In these cases, long term job security is traded for a significant increase in salary, perhaps 20-30%.

For the CEOs as an interest group (and for the national associations of CEOs), job security constitutes a significant area of interest. In countries such as Denmark, where the frequency of non-voluntary derecruitment is increasing, the protection of the interests of the CEOs in these cases constitutes a highly prioritized item on the agenda of their professional associations.

In a theoretical perspective, de-recruitment is important because we can learn much about organizations by studying the specific nature of the bond between organizations and their staff. In Weber's classical bureaucracy, for instance, job security is one of the key defining features. The professional bureaucrat, in Weber's words, is 'chained to his activity by his entire material and ideal existence' (Weber 1946, 228). The particular type of bond in bureaucratic organizations enhances a whole set of values congruent with bureaucracy, including loyalty and predictability. Weber quite clearly sees the secure material foundation of the bureaucrat as instrumental in maintaining the loyalty of the bureaucrat towards the larger organizational goals (Weber 1971, 110).

Weber's bureaucracy is a purely conceptual construct. In reality, the nature of the bond between organizations and their employees varies considerably. Nevertheless, with Weber in mind, we can hypothesize that organizations which offer only decreasing or limited degrees of job security may find loyalty and predictability decreasing – unless organizational mechanisms are in place which are, in this respect, functionally equivalent to the job security offered by the practically permanent contract.

Organizing the Bond Between Local Government and the CEO

Several attempts have been made to categorize various forms of local government. Some of the typologies have had a general focus while others have emphasized specific themes. We suggest the following four models to describe the bond between local government and the CEO. Each of these produce different predictions about derecruitment.

Bureaucracy represents a model in which stability and life-long tenure is a key feature. The typical CEO has grown with the municipal system or has at least a long affiliation with local government. Having entered his position, the CEO will stay in the same municipality for the rest of his active career. He will be immune to changes at the political level and will – if not violating any general rule – also have a strong administrative base. The life-time affiliation between local government and the CEO gives a high degree of stability to the political level and to the administration. The CEO, in return for his commitment to the organization, is rewarded with a secure position and a minimal risk of being fired. In a local government system characterized by the bureaucracy model, we can expect a low degree of turnover.

Another model is the pure *market model*. Whereas the dominant feature in the bureaucracy model is stability, flexibility is the key factor in the market model. In general, it is supply and demand which determine hiring and firing. The connection between two parties in a market transaction lasts only as long as both parties do not have a better alternative giving them higher utility. Very few additional factors keep the parties together. If the CEO can obtain a better paid or more prestigious job by moving to another municipality, he is more or less free to do so. Likewise, if the political leadership in a municipality is dissatisfied with the CEO and able to attract another CEO, it will be able to do so without too high costs. This system gives a high degree of flexibility – but also uncertainty – for both parties. In order to limit the uncertainty, time-limited contracts can be used. In its pure form, the market model does not limit the position of CEO to persons with long experience in the municipal system. Candidates with experience from private businesses, voluntary organizations and other government agencies will be able to enter the market for the CEO job. In reality, the 'localness' of the job will favor applicants with some local government background.

In systems characterized by the market model, we can expect a relatively high degree of turnover.

A third model is the *centrally controlled career* model. The key factor of this model is coordination. The career of the local government CEO is determined by decisions made by central government, and the CEO is moved around among local governments. In other words, recruitment and derecruitment is taken out of the hands of the individual CEO as well as the local government. Qualifications required to enter the position, and length of service will also be determined centrally. A centrally controlled system may eliminate the effects of factors otherwise influencing job changes. From a central government point of view, the centrally controlled career model gives some of the same flexibility known from the pure market model. In the centrally controlled career model, we would expect a high degree of turnover.

Party affiliation is a fourth model. The key factor here is a match between the CEO's political belief and the governing coalition. In order to obtain the position as CEO, the right political affiliation is needed. This means that the career of the CEO is dependent upon changes at the political level. The CEO comes and goes with the political leadership. In the centrally controlled career model, the degree of stability is a function of decisions made at upper-level government. In the political affiliation model, it is primarily up to the political leadership in each municipality to determine the turnover, and in systems with fixed terms, the length of the term will also be of importance.

As indicated earlier, the bureaucracy model has had an important impact in several countries. In the three Scandinavian states, this model dominated up through the 1980s. In recent years, however, the market model has become more pronounced in Norway, Sweden and Denmark (Anderson & Pedersen 1998; Baldersheim & Øgård 1999; Haglund 1998). It is especially in turnover we see major changes, but also in terms of a broader background. British local government also shares some of the characteristics of the bureaucracy model. The local government CEO in Britain primarily has his background within local government and does not plan to seek another job (Goldsmith & Tonge 1998). Local Government in the Netherlands, too, has many characteristics of the bureaucracy model. Traces of the market model are also visible here. All in all, the bureaucracy model is challenged by the market model in many countries.

The market model is not found in its pure form in any of the countries in this study. The USA and Australia are somewhat in accordance with the market model, but in both countries huge variations exist between the individual states. In the USA, CEOs in council-manager government used to be generalists moving in and out of various administrative positions in different sectors (Svara 1998). This feature of the market model is to some extent still present, but it is being challenged by careerists who operate primarily within the municipal system (ibid.). In Australia some of the main characteristics of the market model are gaining ground. Due to the influence of 'managerialism', less emphasis is on specific knowledge of local government and more on general managerial qualifications (Gerritsen & Whyard 1998).

It is in the Southern European countries that traces of the centrally controlled career model ('the Napoleonic system') can be found. Italian local government has been especially influenced by centrally controlled career systems moving CEOs between local governments, but also Spain, Portugal and France have some of the same characteristics. During the past decade, however, new rules were passed in most of the countries creating a situation where several features of the different models are combined (Costa, Felizes & Neves 1998; Delgado, Nieto & López 1998; Gamberucci & Magnier 1998; Thoenig & Burlen 1998).

The party affiliation model is not prominent in any of the countries participating in this study, but some traces can be found in Finland. A majority of Finnish local government CEOs are currently members of a political party, and being a member of the same party as the person who hires usually increases a candidate's chances of obtaining the position (Sandberg 1998). However, other features such as a large majority with strong municipal ties point toward the bureaucracy model.

Belgium is a good example of how the different models are mixed. Belgian administrative practice has several characteristics from the bureaucracy model as well as the centrally controlled career system. The centrally controlled rules concerning formal requirements point toward the latter model, while the limited external recruitment, and a generally closed municipal system, point toward the bureaucracy model (Pless & Laurent 1998). All in all, Belgium will be very close to the bureaucracy model.

Analyzing Derecruitment in Local Government

Derecruitment can take several forms and can be a function of several factors. Here we examine two types of derecruitment: career derecruitment and cooperation derecruitment. Both types are playing an increasing role, are theoretically significant and are relatively controversial in practice. (In contrast to these forms of derecruitment, natural derecruitment has been decreasing and is of minor theoretical and practical significance.)

Our dependent variables are:

- *Career derecruitment*: The CEO left the job because of a better paying or more prestigious job elsewhere.
- *Cooperation derecruitment:* The CEO left the job because of problems of cooperation with politicians or bureaucrats.

The two dependent variables are related. A CEO who faces problems of cooperation with his superiors may voluntarily opt for 'career derecruitment', although the factors operating in the situation would rightly have predicted cooperation derecruitment. There is a negative correlation among the three types of derecruitment to the extent that one substitutes for another. However, positive correlations are also possible. The more cooperation derecruitment takes place, the more positions may be open for career derecruitment. In a similar vein, our two types of derecruitment may be related to other types of derecruitment, such as natural derecruitment. Therefore, we cannot identify whether a successful causal explanation of variations in one of our dependent variables strengthens or undermines our explanation of the other.

When trying to explain our two types of derecruitment, we quickly discover a number of explanatory variables which cannot be integrated into a comparative analysis. In the following, we suggest four groups of independent variables, within which a few variables will be selected for further analysis.

Independent variables:

- *Local government systems* and institutional rules, i.e. the four models of the bond between local government and CEO presented earlier.
- The *characteristics of the CEOs* are likely to affect derecruitment patterns. These characteristics range from age and gender to job qualifications, career ambitions, and personal values.
- *Characteristics of the job,* such as the level of conflict and stress, relations to superiors and subordinates, and the role performed by the CEO are likely to affect derecruitment patterns.
- *External pressures* and expectations in the organizational environment probably affect the rate of cooperation derecruitment. Cooperation problems are more likely to occur in situations where external pressure on the organizational system is high.

In sum, we are dealing with a complicated case of causal explanation. There are two interrelated dependent variables and a large number of independent ones (organized under four headings) which may also be interrelated and some of which condition the effects of others.

There are other relevant variables which cannot be elucidated by the available data. For example, a CEO may have a great desire for career and apply for higher-level or better paid jobs, but others will decide whether he/she gets it or not. There is a demand side and a supply side to career moves. We lack good methods of measuring the supply side.

Empirically, there is no direct access to reliable data about the various types of derecruitment. Official records are often non-existent, and if they did, their reliability would be low since underlying conflicts leading to the firing of a CEO are usually not described in official documents.

We base the following analysis on the subjective judgments of present CEOs (in the form of survey data) about the reasons why his or her predecessor left the job. For this reason, we have no access to data about attitudes, motivations and emotions of the person who actually left the job. Moreover, if derecruitment took place long ago, legends, stories and faulty memories may obfuscate our data. Even if a change in CEO took place recently, the present CEO may not know or may not want to report the full story of his/her predecessor's departure. Nevertheless, because of his/her central position on the scene, the present CEO may be a more reliable source of information on this matter than any other available source.

We shall measure each type of derecruitment by the percentage of all CEOs in a country who claim that their predecessor left his/her job due to each particular reason. *Our dependent variables describe the amount of turnover in the total corps of CEOs in each country during the last five years due to each type of derecruitment.* The analysis includes 12 countries which all differ from zero in our dependent variables.

We operate on two levels of analysis. The first is a country-by-country comparison, or 'ecological analysis' as referred to by Hofstede *et al.* (1993, 487). On the second level, we describe within-country differences between municipal organizations. We shall refer to this level as 'organizational' since we have only one CEO from each organization, and he/she describes the organizational setting rather than his/her predecessor in person.

At the organizational level, we shall be deducting the national average of any explanatory variable from the individual scores in order to rule out national differences from our organizational comparisons. This is what Hofstede *et al.* (1993, 487) refers to as an 'individual analysis'. Note that since differences between national averages are excluded from the individual analysis, this type of analysis is completely separate from and not overlapping with the country-by-country comparison (Hofstede *et al.* 1993, 487).

Great care should therefore be taken in the definition of our explanatory variables. A variable meaningful at one level may have a different meaning or none at all at a different level of analysis. Local government systems, for instance, vary between countries, but not between municipalities in a country. They are properties of nations, not organizations. Consider the more complicated example of the degree of 'conflict' between CEOs and politicians. At the organizational level, career derecruitment may increase when conflict is perceived to be lower in an alternative organization where one may wish to apply for a job. If the level of conflict is an inherent property of the particular institutional set-up within a country, however, one cannot escape from this factor by moving from one organization to another within the same country (we assume that mobility of CEOs between countries is negligible). If the CEOs do not have illusions about a lower level of conflict in other organizations in the same country, the conflict variable does not explain differences in derecruitment between countries. Yet conflict may be a very relevant variable at the organizational/individual level.

In other words, different levels of analysis demand that we account for each variable in different ways. In the following, we shall analyze those variables which can best explain variations in the two types of derecruitment at national and organizational levels.

Career Derecruitment
Explaining Career Derecruitment at the National Level

Characteristics of the Local Government System

Characteristics of the local government system are assumed to have a direct influence on career derecruitment. We will also investigate the number of municipalities in the country and the variation in size, based on the assumption that it will influence the possibilities of obtaining a higher or better paid job.

Looking at figure 9.1, Italy is exceptional due to a high career derecruitment score. This is probably due to traces of the 'Napoleonic system', a centrally controlled career system. The other countries have a much lower score. However, considering the influence of the bureaucracy model, in which leaders once appointed remain for the rest of their careers, we would expect only a minimum or no career derecruitment. Using this as a yardstick, the level of career derecruitment is higher than expected. The many reforms in local government in Western countries carried out during the past two decades have probably had an influence on the level of career derecruitment. Some of the reforms have been aimed directly at the bureaucratic nature of the local government organization, e.g., many of the reforms inspired by New Public Management have introduced fixed-time contracts, thus creating a more dynamic system.

Figure 9.1: Predecessors who left due to career advancement within five years.

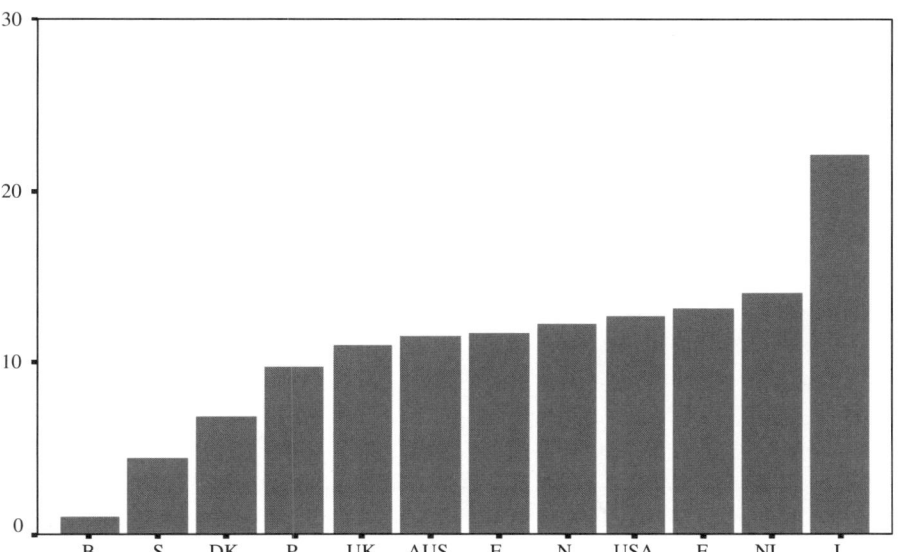

Some countries have changed their entire local government systems by amalgamating municipalities or alternating formal structures, work procedures, etc. within the municipality. This applies even to reforms not aimed directly at changing career patterns. These changes can thus be seen as a movement towards the market model. That career derecruitment has increased notably can be seen as the first opening in the local government career system. On the other hand, the limited proportion of career derecruitment clearly indicates that the career systems in local government do not change overnight. The CEO position is to a large extent still the highest position to which one can rise, and the CEO is not easily pulled away. Despite the reforms and new principles for hiring and firing, the bureaucracy model shows its influence and resistance towards change.

The variation in size between municipalities within the country is also expected to influence career derecruitment. If we concentrate on career moves between municipalities, the variation in size can play an important role. If all municipalities had about the same size, it would limit the possibilities of making career moves within the system, as opposed to systems with larger variation where moves from one municipality to another would be considered a career advancement. However, looking at figure 9.2, this is not the case. No strong relationship can be detected between career derecruitment and variation in sizes of municipalities (measured as the standard deviation). To understand this, we may turn to the supply side of the market. If CEOs in large municipalities leave only for natural reasons, then the turnover in the whole system becomes relatively slow. There is not a sufficient number of jobs available for the career-oriented CEOs in small municipalities.

Figure 9.2: Career derecruitment and variation in sizes of municipalities.

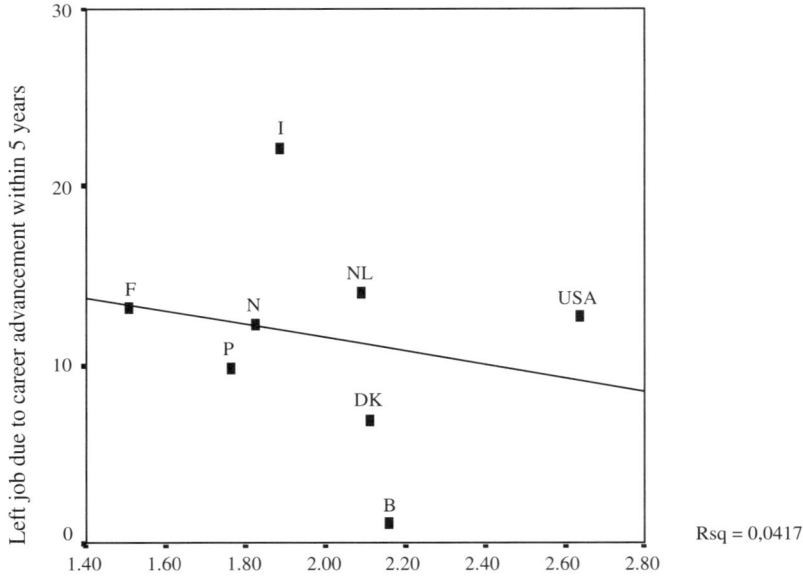

Part of the explanation for the missing relation between career derecruitment and variation in sizes of municipalities may be attributed to certain characteristics of the local government system. In countries with federal systems, the job market may be reduced to the individual state, thus reducing mobility. The same applies to types of municipal systems such as that in USA, where CAOs may apply for a CEO position but not the other way around (Svara 1998). In low-scoring Belgium, there are also restrictions on how CEOs may apply for the most prestigious jobs in the large cities. One would expect that career derecruitment would be closely connected to the desire to seek another job sometime in the future. At first glance, this is not the case. However, if Italy is excluded from the analysis, we find a stronger relationship between career derecruitment and the desire for career. As previously discussed, the Italian career system was centrally controlled. For this reason, it is justified to exclude Italy in this particular analysis. With Italy excluded, figure 9.3 shows a clear relationship between career derecruitment and the desire for career. The figure should be interpreted with care, however. Since preferences and aspirations are socially constructed (Meyer, Boli & Thomas 1987) CEOs may partly shape their career desires in light of what is possible within their institutional contexts.

Two other sets of CEO characteristics, the proportion who are academics and their average age, are expected to influence career derecruitment. The hypothesis is that academics are more inclined to seek new positions (consistent with deHoog & Whitaker 1990) and, due to their academic background, will have greater opportunities to pursue careers outside the local government system. Based on the available data, the hypothesis cannot be confirmed.

Figure 9.3: Career derecruitment and desire for career.

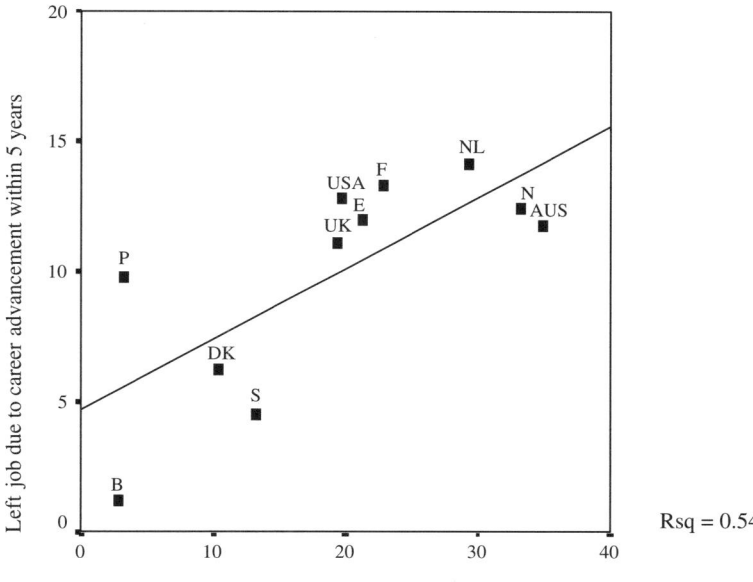

The average age is expected to be negatively correlated with career derecruitment. However, this hypothesis cannot be supported by the data, either. The fact that great age leads to natural derecruitment which again creates more vacancies for career makers may partly explain this.

Career Derecruitment and the Job as CEO

Variations in the job content of the CEOs' work can be described in terms of various emphases on certain job roles or dimensions. The hypothesis is that local government systems with emphasis on the classical management dimension will show less career derecruitment. The classical management dimension may be strongly connected to bureaucratic types of organizations where lifetime attachment to the organizations is more likely. Looking at figure 9.4, the hypothesis cannot be confirmed. The opposite relationship seems to be the case – the higher the score on the classical management dimension, the more career derecruitment. This pattern could be a function of the Napoleonic tradition. Figure 9.4 reveals a north-south pattern, with the southern countries reporting high scores on the classical management function and high or medium scores on career derecruitment.[1] These countries have a very centralized system with low municipal autonomy, which in turn encourages the classical management dimension. At the same time, remnants from the Napoleonic tradition result in higher mobility.

Explaining Career Derecruitment at the Organizational Level

The available data limit our ability to analyze career derecruitment at the organizational/individual level. We cannot describe the person who actually left the job, since derecruitment is described only through the eyes of the subsequent CEO. Nevertheless, we have one set of data – the size of municipalities – that can help us analyze career derecruitment. We assume that career derecruitment takes place more often from small municipalities than from large municipalities. This is the case in the Southern European countries (France, Spain, Portugal and Italy, data not shown). Again, it is relevant to point to the Napoleonic tradition in these countries. Career moves are more blurred across different sizes of municipalities in the other countries. In a country such as Belgium, such career moves are restricted by rules.

---

[1] The 'classical management' index is based on the question 'Chief executives must necessarily decide the priority of various tasks. Please indicate how much emphasis you put on each of the tasks listed below in your daily work'. Classical management includes the following items: 'Guide subordinate staff in day-to-day handling of cases'; 'Develop and implement new routines and work methods'; 'Manage economic affairs, accounts and budgetary control' and 'Ensure that rules and regulations are followed'.

Figure 9.4: Career derecruitment and classical managers.

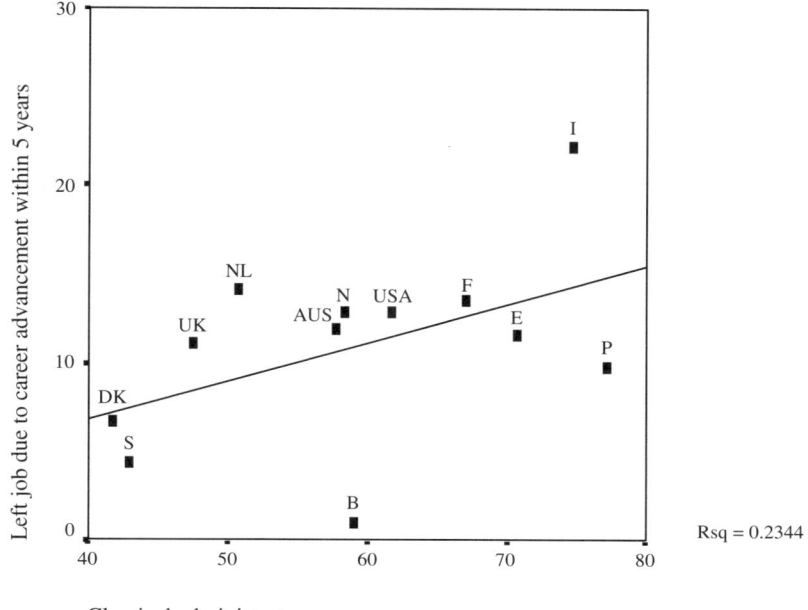

Cooperation Derecruitment
Explaining Cooperation Derecruitment at the National Level

Characteristics of the CEOs
We assume that cultural variables such as individualism and uncertainty avoidance help explain variations in the amount of cooperation derecruitment across countries. Data (not shown) do not support this assumption.

The Job as CEO

Variations in the CEO's level of conflict with the mayor as well as with other significant actors are hypothesized to help explain variations in cooperation derecruitment across countries. However, there are clear indications of a negative relation between conflict level and cooperation derecruitment not only in relation to the mayor, but to other actors as well (data not shown).

Perhaps these apparently counterintuitive data can be explained. The significance of a particular conflict depends on how much one depends on the actor with whom one is in conflict. And since dependence and conflict are negatively related (you avoid conflict with those on whom you depend), the surprising, negative association between conflict and derecruitment occurs. Dependency may thus be a better predictor of cooperation derecruitment than conflict. Figure 9.5 indicates a positive relationship between the CEO's dependence on politicians other than the mayor and cooperation derecruitment. Especially striking is the United States which scores very high on both variables. The fact that city managers in the US are hired 'at the will' of the city council may help explain the high frequency of cooperation derecruitment in this country.

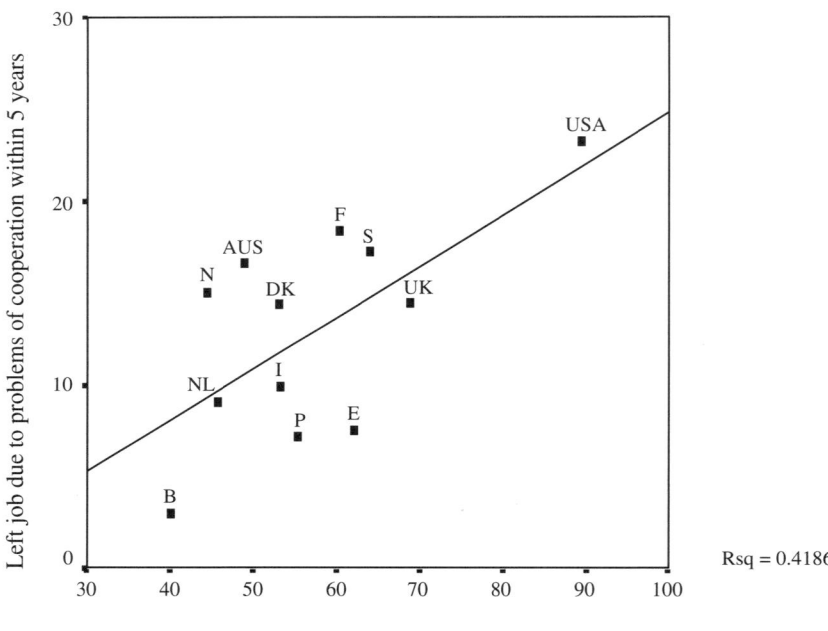

Figure 9.5: Problems of cooperation and dependency.

The role played by the CEO on the job may have an impact on derecruitment patterns. According to our typology of 'dimensions' in the tasks performed, the role of 'classical bureaucrat' may be relatively safe, whereas the 'entrepreneur' may play a more risky role.[2] The entrepreneur initiates unconventional projects and more often enters the grey zone between politics and administration. Figure 9.6 supports the hypothesis that the more CEOs play an entrepreneurial role, the higher the risk of

---

[2] The 'entrepeneur' index is based on the same main question as the 'classical management' index, but includes the following items: 'Formulate ideas and visions' and 'Promote and encourage new projects in the community.'

cooperation derecruitment. It is not implied here that the choice of the role of 'entrepreneur' is an independent choice of the individual CEO (recall that data are displayed at the country level). The high score on the entrepreneurial dimension in Denmark, Sweden and the Anglo-Saxon countries reflects the fact that in these countries, local governments play a relatively active policy-shaping role. The implication for CEOs is that they may have a chance to expand on the more innovative and experimental dimensions in their job. To be an entrepreneur, however, is sometimes risky business.

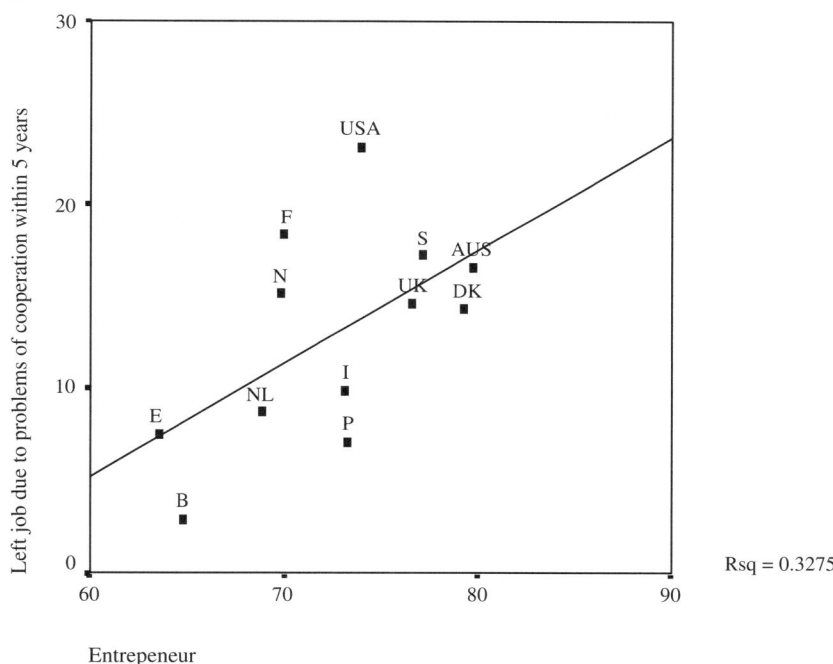

Figure 9.6: Problems of cooperation and the role of the CEOs.

External pressures

We sometimes best understand organizational processes in relation to broader forces in the organizational environment. The concluding set of hypotheses in this section thus suggests that cooperation derecruitment is more frequent in those countries where the CEO reports about external pressures, such as social problems, local organized interests, and demands from citizens.[3]

---

[3] The survey question was phrased: 'To what extent has your ability to perform your job as chief executive been affected *negatively* by the following factors during recent years?'

Graphs illustrating the three factors are displayed in figures 9.7-9.9.

Figure 9.7: Problems of cooperation and negative factors I

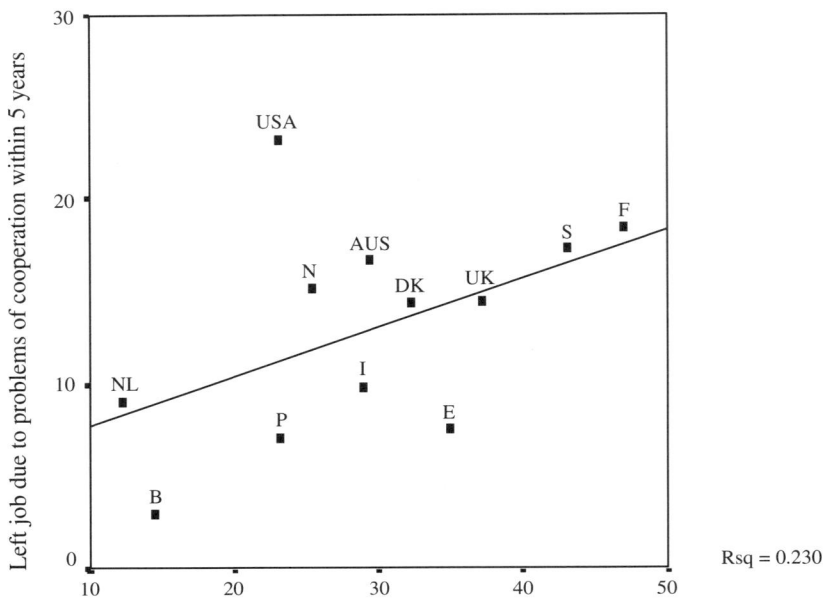

All the scattergrams indicate positive relationships between a particular type of external pressure on the municipal system and cooperation derecruitment. Note also that as we move from broad problems to more specific pressures from specific actors, the more the countries in the scattergram conform to a straight and steep line. In other words, it is not *amorphous challenges or threats in the environment, but specific political demands on the political-administrative system made by specific groups that indicate the type of pressure which best explains cooperation derecruitment.* This adds credibility to the idea that as specific interests exert more pressure on the municipal system, the more challenging and difficult becomes the job as a municipal CEO.

External pressures may raise the level of expectations, lower the threshold of incompetency and inaction accepted and simply make it more difficult to be a CEO. External pressures may perhaps make the role of entrepreneur more relevant and demanding, and we have seen that this role seemed to be more risky in terms of cooperation derecruitment.

It may also be the case that the problems in the organizational environments themselves are not decisive for the CEOs. The data in this section describe whether the

Figure 9.8: Problems of cooperation and negative factors II

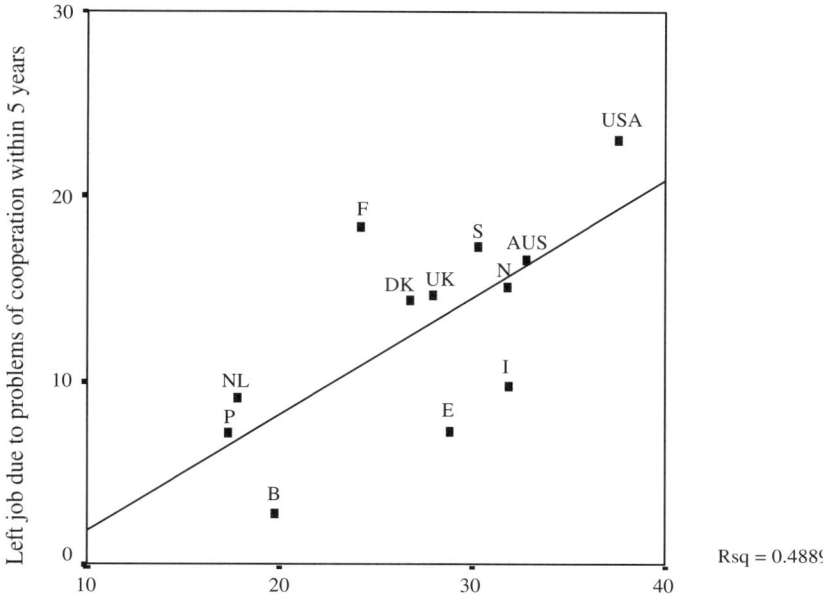

Pressures from local organized interests, etc.

CEO perceives external pressures as having negatively affected his/her ability to perform as a CEO. It is possible that this pressure is *felt* more in countries where local governments have a broad range of responsibilities for handling policy areas where social problems and demands for better service are salient. We are measuring not only the pressures as such, but also the sensitivity of local government towards these kinds of pressures. Or in the terminology of neo-institutional organization theory (DiMaggio & Powell 1991), the key factor is the extent to which the legitimacy of the municipal system depends on its ability to handle particular external pressures.

The various definitions of the role of local government in society form the background against which the findings in this section should be understood.

Explaining Cooperation Derecruitment at the Organizational Level

We turn now to the organizational/individual level of analysis. Our dependent variable is thus a dummy variable. Cooperation derecruitment either occurred or did not occur in each municipal organization. Our independent variables have all been re-coded into three categories 'over', 'at' or 'below' the national average, thus allowing what Hofstede *et al.* calls a truly 'individual' analysis (Hofstede *et al.* 1993).

Figure 9.9: Problems of cooperation and negative factors III

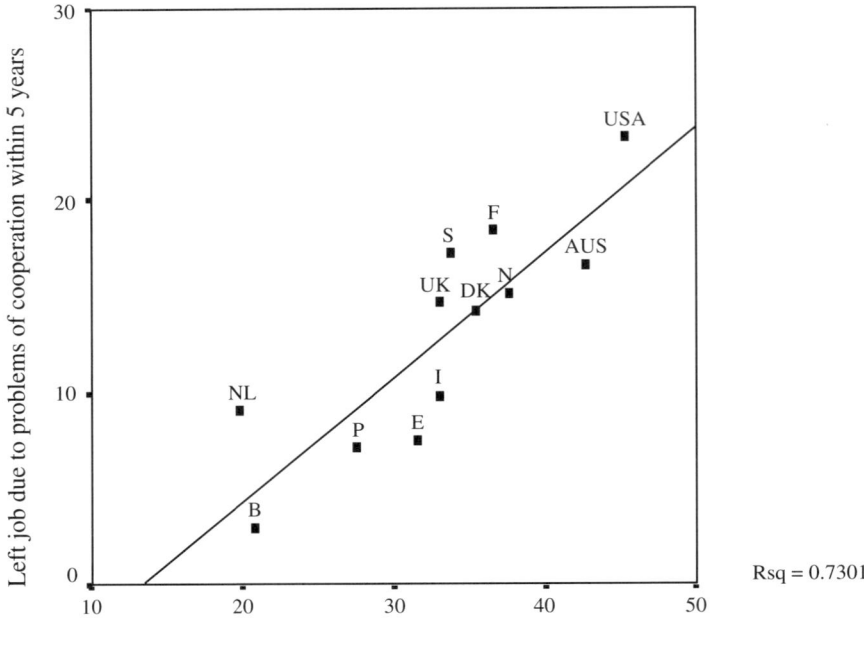

Remember that our data reveal nothing about the CEO who has left the job. We know only how the present CEO describes life in the organization from which his predecessor departed. In other words, the 'characteristics of the CEOs' are ruled out from our analysis. The same is true for 'institutional rules', since we are not comparing countries. This leaves us with internal problems on the job and with external pressures as independent variables.

Internal problems

In the following, we assume that the present CEO's description of the organization and the job reveals genuine characteristics of the municipal organization which were more or less the same up to five years earlier when there was another CEO (we avoid reporting data on stress and other person-specific factors which are not likely to meet this criteria).

Table 9.1 describes whether over-the-national-average scores on items such as conflicts and other potential sources of frustration are significantly related to the predecessor having departed due to cooperation problems.

Leaving the Job as CEO

Table 9.1: Significance of correlations between various factors and cooperation derecruitment.

Conflict with mayor *
Conflict with other politicians
Conflict with opposition
Conflict with heads of departments *
Conflict with other employees
Conflict with other CEOs
Conflict with citizens*
Conflict with regional gov. officials*
Conflict with central gov. officials
Conflict with other public officials*
Conflicts with unions regarding salaries*
Conflicts with unions regarding other issues
Conflicts with business interests*
Affected negatively by conflicts between pol. parties*
Affected negatively by lack of clear political goals
Affected negatively by conflicts between various departments or department heads*
Affected negatively by unclear division of labour between politicians and administration*
Affected negatively by financial problems in the municipality

* = significant at $p < 0.01$ (one-sided test).

In contrast to what we found at the national level, various measures of conflict clearly help explain cooperation derecruitment. Conflict with the mayor, with heads of departments, with citizens, with various officials, with unions and business officials all predict cooperation derecruitment. In addition, the same is true when conflicts between political parties, between department heads and an unclear division of labour between politicians and the administration negatively affect the CEO's ability to perform his/her job.

External Pressures

It is quite logical that as the organization is felt to be under an extraordinary pressure, it may be more difficult for the CEO to avoid cooperation problems which threaten his job security. Among the external pressures which affect the CEO's ability to perform, new regulations from upper-level government, central control of municipal finances, and pressures from local organized interests help explain differences in cooperation derecruitment between municipalities. When these factors are reported to be above the national average in a particular municipaly, perhaps because there is already financial strain in the municipality, the likelihood of cooperation derecruitment among CEOs increases.

Table 9.2: Significance of correlations between various factors negatively affecting the job as CEO and cooperation derecruitment.

new regulations from upper-level government*
demands from the population for better service
demographic changes
central control of local government finances*
unemployment and social problems
cuts in grants from upper-level government
pressures from local organized interests, business etc. *

* = significant at $p < 0.01$ (one-sided test).

Some of the factors in table 9.2 such as demographic changes which do not exert a significant influence on cooperation derecruitment may be more or less general pressures on the whole field of municipalities in a country rather than organization-specific factors.

Conclusion

In trying to explain patterns of derecruitment, we have embarked upon a difficult undertaking. The involved causal links are complex, several apparently self-evident hypotheses were not supported, and much of what we would like to know is still not covered by data.

Yet a few hypotheses have gained credibility as a result of our analysis.

Career derecruitment depends largely on local government systems and institutional rules. Italy's high score can be accounted for in terms of remnants of the centrally controlled career system. Apart from Italy, the aspirations of the whole corps of CEOs seem to make a difference.

Factors at the individual and organizational levels were largely unable to explain career derecruitment. At these levels, we probably lack the decisive data which might have helped us explain individual career moves, since we rely on the newly appointed CEO rather than the resigned CEO as our source of data. Despite the scarcity of clear results, our analysis of career derecruitment has compelled us to consider the 'labour market' for CEOs as a highly institutionalized phenomenon which, in many countries, does not resemble the characteristics of an open market.

We were somewhat more successful in explaining cooperation derecruitment. *In countries where the organizational environment (organizations, business interests and local citizens) exerts pressure on local government, it becomes more difficult to successfully fulfil the role as CEO. Consequently, the cooperation derecruitment is more frequent.* Largely overlapping with these countries, there are countries in which *the CEO plays an extensive entrepreneurial role, which in itself also seems to lead to increased cooperation derecruitment.* In such countries as the US, Australia, the UK, Denmark and Sweden, CEOs feel the external pressures more than others, and they also play the entrepreneurial role more extensively. When the role and function of local government include the responsibility to deal with such pressures, CEOs become more entrepreneurial, and their rate of cooperation derecruitment is higher.

Conflict in the municipal system also helps explain cooperation derecruitment. The general level of conflict in a country has not been demonstrated to be interesting, but *organizations with a higher-than-national-average level of conflict produce significantly more cooperation derecruitment than other organizations.* The conflicts may concern the CEO's relations to the mayor, to external and internal officials and bureaucrats as well as to external actors such as citizens, trade unions and business interests. The level of conflict *between* other actors also affects the rate of cooperation derecruitment for the CEOs.

These results are hardly surprising. What is surprising, however, is that the level of conflict can be measured up to five years after the departure of the former CEO and continues to constitute a significant explanatory factor. The level of conflict we measure is thus a truly *organizational* phenomenon rather than a socio-psychological one.

We have found that *both institutional factors and external pressures on the municipal systems help explain differences in derecruitment patterns across countries. On this general background, differences in levels of organizational conflict within a country can help explain why CEOs leave one organization rather than another one within a country.*

We offer the following speculation for the future: If, as a result of increased pressure on local governments, CEOs play a more active and entrepreneurial role, conventional bureaucratic arrangements may be challenged. In the long run, these arrangements may be loosened, leading to more short-term contracts, and to more derecruitment due to factors other than the natural ones. In this situation, CEOs may search for new institutional arrangements to protect their interests, or perhaps opt for the higher salary which sometimes goes hand-in-hand with short term and more risky employment conditions. Some countries have already gone a long way down this path.

In other countries, more conventional, traditionally bureaucratic patterns are institutionally maintained. These may be stable, especially if the role and obligation of central government in society is more limited and there is less need to respond to new pressures. If a conventional institutional pattern of hiring (and not firing) is maintained while new tasks and roles are taken up, it is possible that conflicts will surface, perhaps in some organizations more than others. A problem inherent in a national institutional arrangement will thus take the form of an organizational problem. These speculations suggest that the numerous interacting factors explaining patterns of derecruitment will make the interplay between levels of analysis both complicated and delicate.

Methodological Appendix

BY PETER DAHLER-LARSEN, POUL ERIK MOURITZEN, STEFFEN PETERSEN AND MIKAEL SØNDERGAARD

Contents

1. The survey
2. The interviews
3. The job postings
4. The calculation of indices

The Survey

A joint questionnaire was prepared during 1995. In January of that year, the first joint meeting among the researchers was held in Odense, Denmark. At the meeting, the terms for the project and the survey were decided. During the following months, the Odense team prepared a draft of the questionnaire, which was presented and discussed at a meeting in Bordeaux, France, at the end of April. The comments and ideas from the Bordeaux meeting were implemented during the Summer, and the first surveys were carried out by the end of 1995. From November 1995 until May 1997, 14 countries conducted the survey. The questionnaire in toto is reproduced in Klausen and Magnier (1998, 292-311).

The joint questionnaire consists of 54 core questions resulting in 254 variables. Each country was allowed to add country specific questions. These questions, however, are not part of the joint datafile.

The third joint project meeting was held in Odense in January 1996. At this meeting a coding workshop was conducted involving student assistants from nine countries. During the week in Odense, the coders participated in the development of general coding principles as well as in the development of categories for open-ended questions. The coders were very competent and returned to their countries to finish the job in an efficient way, guided by the common principles. Countries which did not participate in the coding workshop received individual advice about how to code the questionnaires and how to work with the datafile.

Information about the survey from each of the 14 countries is given in the table below. The response rates vary considerably across countries.

Table 1: Response rates.

Country	Survey conducted	Sent out	Returned	Response rate	Comments on population
Australia	Oct 96	670	246	37	All local governments with the exception of Aboriginal community governments in the Northern Territory
Belgium	Nov-Dec 95	589	351	60	All municipalities are included in the survey. Questionnaire mailed in both a Dutch and a French version
Denmark	Nov 95	275	200	73	All Danish municipalities
Finland	March-April 96	439	308	70	All municipalities except those of the Åland Islands
France	Dec 95-Jan 96	772	266	35	A stratified disproportionate sampling drawn among municipalities with more than 5000 inhabitants.
The Netherlands	March-May 96	584	404	69	All municipalities, except 59 which do not have an appointed CEO
Ireland	May-June 96	34	21	62	All municipalities are included
Italy	Dec 95-March 96	2000	541	27	Italy has 8,100 municipalities, but only 6,100 CEOs. Several CEOs work in two or three small municipalities. The sample is 50 pct. of all municipalities with more than 10,000 inhabitants, and 50 pct. of a random sample of municipalities with less than 10,000 inhabitants
Norway	Jan 97	434	325	75	All municipalities are included
Portugal	Dec 95	275	104	38	All municipalities except the Islands of Madeira and the Azores
Spain	Nov 95	5000	366	7	The actual population is 8,120. Questionnaire distributed with newsletter to CEOs
Sweden	Nov-Dec 95	279	224	80	The actual population is 288, but 9 municipalities did not have an appointed CEO at the time
The UK	Dec 95-Feb 96	511	284	56	Total population less City of London
USA	Jan-May 97	1178	697	59	CEO/CAO in all cities with more than 50,000 inhabitants and a sample of one quarter of the cities with a population between 2,500-50,000.

In order to increase the representativeness of the samples, weights have been created along two dimensions. The first dimension takes care of the problem with representativeness within each country with regard to municipal size. The second dimension takes care of the differences between the countries with regard to sample size. In creating the weights a special problem concerning the many small

Methodological Appendix

municipalities in the Southern European countries occurred. In France, no questionnaires were sent to municipalities with less than 5,000 inhabitants. Italy also has a lot of small municipalities. Several CEOs work in more than one municipality. Only a few of these were included in the Italian data. In Spain, however, the questionnaire was distributed with a newsletter to the CEOs, and since the majority of municipalities have less than 2,000 inhabitants, most of the responses came from these small municipalities.

In the present book, all analyses are based on weighted data. When the weights are used, all Spanish municipalities with a population less than 2,000 and all Italian municipalities with a population less than 2,000 were excluded from the sample.

Interviews

To get a more detailed knowledge of the work of a CEO, a series of intensive interviews were conducted in some of the participating countries (cf. table 2). Most of the interviews were recorded and transcribed. In some cases, English summaries were made and distributed among participants.

Table 2: Number of intensive interviews conducted.

Country	Number of interviews
Denmark	3 (+15 in previous study)
The UK	7
France	17
The Netherlands	6
Ireland	6
Norway	21
Portugal	2
USA	5 (incl. two former mayors)

All interviews were based on an interview guide according to which the following items/questions were covered:

1. INTRODUCTION.
    1.1. Presentation of the U.Di.T.E project
    1.2. Issues of anonymity, how data are dealt with
    1.3 Plans of publication (broadly)
    1.4 Questions raised by interviewee

2. BACKGROUND (some of these items can be filled in by the researcher, just make sure all are registered)
    2.1. Country, age, gender
    2.2. Career background
    2.3. Characterization of municipality as area
    2.4. Characterization of municipality as administrative structure
    2.5. What are the most important recent problems in the municipality (external and internal)?

3. JOB AS CEO
    3.1. How would you broadly characterize your job as a city manager?
    (Tasks, dilemmas, problems, opportunities, cross pressures, predictability, active/reactive, external relations, rules/administration versus entrepreneurship, leader versus manager, fire-fighting?)

4. RELATION TO POLITICS/POLITICIANS IN GENERAL
    4.1. How would you describe the general political climate in the municipality?
    (conflict? stability? fixed majority? who runs things?)
    4.2. What are the effects of this climate on your role as CEO?
    4.3. How would you describe the ideal politician seen from your position?
    (related to: ideal definition of politics versus administration)
    4.4. How and to what extent do the politicians differ from this ideal?
    4.5. Effects thereof on role as CEO
    4.6. Any attempts by CEO to influence style/behaviour of politicians?

5. RELATION TO MAJORITY/ MINORITY
    5.1. Please describe broadly your relations to both political majority and minority
    5.2. Effects of majority/minority issues on role as CEO

6. RELATION TO MAYOR
    6.1. How would you broadly characterize the mayor?
    (relation to voters, to party, to entire political body)
    6.2. Please describe the division of tasks between the mayor and the CEO
    6.3. Please describe the type of advice you may give the mayor
    6.4. What are the effects of your relation to the mayor on your role as a CEO

Job Postings

The term 'job posting' refers to advertisements that provide information about a municipal vacancy. Job postings typically describe the job content, professional and personal qualification requirements etc. This information is – in contradiction to sur-

Methodological Appendix 141

vey data – typically independent of the perspective of the person who actually performs the CEO job. Job postings are also used to create or sustain certain public impressions of the particular municipality and its administration. On the other hand, job postings are not purely symbolic. They may reveal a discourse which helps define standards of municipal leadership.

Of the many countries in the U.Di.T.E. project only those meeting the following criteria could be included in the job posting analysis:

- a researcher in each country would find all or most job postings for municipal CEOs available in one or a few journals in the country
- the design and content of job postings should not be so strictly regulated by central authorities or others that the municipal job postings would be very uniform.

Obviously, these criteria indicate that *the very availability of 'interesting' data for the job posting analysis is in itself an indicator of certain institutional arrangements in each country*. If vacancies are filled on the basis of clientilism, or if recruitment and recruitment processes are determined by central government, there is no need for job postings that make the vacancy publicly known and differentiate between municipalities.

Participants in the job posting analysis were: Denmark, Sweden, Norway, UK, Finland, the Netherlands, and France. In large countries, job postings were randomly sampled. In smaller countries all job postings within specific periods were collected. In order to map historical variations, job postings were selected from three different periods (with slight national variations due to practical circumstances):

– 1975
– 1985
– October 1, 1994 through September 30, 1995.

The 579 job postings were coded with respect to the following eight main categories (involving 77 variables per job posting):

1. Identification (country, year, etc.).
2. The specific add in total (size, number of words, illustrations, logos).
3. Job content and functions.
4. Abilities, experience, formal qualifications.
5. Personal qualifications.
6. Job benefits, salary, terms.
7. Municipality as area.
8. Municipality as administrative organisation.

The job postings were content analysed according to a joint coding scheme. The coding work was carried out by one or two students from each country. A large part of

Table 3: Number of job postings per country and period.

	1970s	1980s	1990s	Cases in total
Denmark	23	39	35	97
Finland	35	36	25	96
France	15	39	59	113
The Netherlands	38	53	24	115
Norway	1	9	40	50
Sweden	16	16	32	64
The UK	25	-	19	44
Cases in total	153	192	234	579

the coding was carried out at a joint coding session in order to clarify both semantic differences and technical problems.

Two methodological choices are central to content analysis, ie. the unit of analysis and the system of renumeration (Holsti 1969, 116ff). Apart from a description of the ad itself, the analysis was based on two different combinations of unit of analysis and renumeration. First, *sentences* were classified according to the above categories. The *number of words* in sentences within categories were then *counted*. Secondly, *themes* were defined within each of the above categories. Each theme was coded as *present or non-present* in the ad. This was determined not on the basis of a simple registration of the particular word (which varies across languages), but on the basis of the coder's educated judgment of the data. For instance, to be 'leader of a team of leaders' was coded as equal to 'leader of a group of leaders'. This element of judgment on the part of each national coder was introduced to enhance the validity of the coding, although reliability could be negatively affected. Where possible, two coders worked on the same data to reduce reliability problems.

In comparative analysis it is, of course, of utmost importance to be aware of the possible inherent cultural biases in the selection of categories. This bias was reduced by

- consulting publications concerning analyses of job postings from more than one country
- discussing the coding scheme among the involved group of international researchers
- integrating suggested categories from various researchers and coders from various countries into the coding scheme.

In addition, one should be aware of the immense difficulties in determining whether a coded item is actually 'the same' across linguistic and cultural borders and, as a corollary, whether the non-occurrence of a particular theme in the job postings in a particular country may be due to the research design's inability to 'catch' that particular property for purely semantic reasons.

The problem was handled through quite intense communication between the author and the coder in the different countries. In addition, the most important analyses rely on more than a single measure of the phenomenon to be analyzed.

The job postings from 1995 were matched one by one to survey questionnaires. This could only be done in countries where standardized rules of ethical conduct in data management as well as practical conditions permitted to do so, ie. in Denmark, the Netherlands, Norway and Finland, but not in France, the UK and Sweden. In other words, this part of the analysis allows us to combine the municipal CEO's own evaluation of his job with the job posting that made him apply for his present job (unless there had been a very recent change of CEOs).

The Calculation of Indices

Many of the questions posed in the survey involved five response categories. In order to simplify the presentation of the results, indices taking values from 0 to 100 were constructed. An example illustrates this procedure. The CEOs were asked to indicate how much emphasis they assigned to different tasks in their daily work. They were also asked to respond on a scale going from 'of utmost importance', 'very important', 'moderate importance', 'little importance' to 'very little or no importance'. In order to simplify the comparison among countries, while still taking the answer from every single respondent into account, the index method was used. If a respondent had answered 'of utmost importance', he was assigned a value of 100, the answer 'very important' was given a value of 75, 'moderate importance' a value of 50, 'of little importance' a value of 25, and if the respondent had answered 'of very little or no importance', he was assigned the value 0. Based on these figures, national averages were calculated.

The calculation of the power distance index (PDI) and uncertainty avoidance index (UAI) is based on the Values Survey Module 1994 (VSM 94) as documented in Hofstede (1994c). The VSM 94 was used with permission from the Institute for Research on Intercultural Cooperation (IRIC). The VSM 94 allows computing scores on five dimensions of national cultures on the basis of four items per dimension. The items used and the exact weighting of each item are based on research experience over a 25-year-period from replication studies of the original IBM study. The 20 items have produced five independent factors which vary across countries. The five cultural dimensions are found only in analyses with countries as units of analysis and they are statistically independent only in the complete set of countries sampled by Hofstede. The 14 countries covered by the U.Di.T.E. Leadership Study are a subset of Hofstede's original sample.

The index formula for calculating the power distance index (PDI) is:

$$\text{PDI} = -\text{cpdi}_1 * (\text{mv1}) + \text{cpdi}_2 * (\text{mv2}) + \text{cpdi}_3 * (\text{mv3}) - \text{cpdi}_4 * (\text{mv4}) - \text{cpdi}_5$$

where cpdi_{1-5} are constants and mv1-4 stand for the country mean scores on the following four variables:

v1: In choosing an ideal job, how important would it be to you to have a good working relationship with your direct superior (five-point scale from 1 (of utmost importance) to 5 (of very little importance)).

v2: In choosing an ideal job, how important would it be to you to be consulted by your direct superior in his/her decisions (five-point scale from 1 (of utmost importance) to 5 (of very little importance)).

v3: How frequently, in your experience, are subordinates afraid to express disagreement with their superiors (five-point scale from 1 (very seldom) to 5 (very frequently)).

v4: To what extent do you agree or disagree with the following statement: An organization structure in which subordinates have two bosses should be avoided (five-point scale from 1 (strongly agree) to 5 (strongly disagree)).

The index formula for calculating the uncertainty avoidance index (UAI) is:

$$\text{UAI} = \text{cuai}_1 * (\text{mv5}) + \text{cuai}_2 * (\text{mv6}) - \text{cuai}_3 * (\text{mv7}) - \text{cuai}_4 * (\text{mv8}) + \text{cuai}_5$$

where cuai_{1-5} are constants and mv5-8 stand for the country mean scores on the following four variables:

v5: How often do you feel nervous or tense at work (five-point scale from 1 (never) to 5 (always)).

v6: To what extent to you agree or disagree with the following statement: One can be a good manager without having precise answers to most questions that subordinates may raise about their work (five-point scale from 1 (strongly agree) to 5 (strongly disagree)).

v7: To what extent to you agree or disagree with the following statement: Competition between employees usually does more harm than good (five-point scale from 1 (strongly agree) to 5 (strongly disagree)).

Methodological Appendix

v8: To what extent to you agree or disagree with the following statement: A company's or organization's rules should not be broken – not even when the employee thinks it is in the company's best interest (five-point scale from 1 (strongly agree) to 5 (strongly disagree)).

Other indices were constructed in a similar way. The indices will normally have a value between 0 (small power distance) and 100 (large power distance); but values below 0 and above 100 are technically possible. For all practical purposes, the U.Di.T.E. scores reproduce Hofstede's original values.

For further details on the construction of indices, see the technical appendix in Svara and Mouritzen (2001).

Participants in the U.Di.T.E. Leadership Study

Australia:	Rolf Gerritsen, Michelle Whyard, Australien Centre of Regional and Local Government Studies, University of Canberra
Belgium:	Thierry Laurent, Rudolf Maes, Yves Plees, Department of Politieke Wetenschappen, Katholieke Universiteit Leuven, Kristof De Leemans, Flemish Fund for Scientific Research, University of Antwerp
Denmark:	Lene Anderson, Peter Dahler-Larsen, Niels Ejersbo, Morten Balle Hansen, Kurt Klaudi Klausen, Poul Erik Mouritzen, Department of Political Science and Public Management, SDU, Odense University. Mikael Søndergaard, Department of Organization and Management, SDU, Odense University
England:	Michael Goldsmith, Jon Tonge, Department of Politics and Contemporary History, Salford University
Finland:	Sari Pikkala, Siv Sandberg, Krister Ståhlberg, Department of Public Administation, Åbo Akademi
France:	Katherine Burlen, Jean Claude Thoenig, GAPP (Groupe d'Analyse des Politiques Publiques), Cachan
Ireland:	Andy Asquith, Department of Politics and Public Policy, University of Luton. Eunan O'Halpin, Dublin City University Business School
Israel:	Nahum Ben-Elia, Policy Analysis, Strategic Urban Planning, Rehovet
Italy:	Maurizio Gamberucci, Annick Magnier, Dipartimento di Scienza della Politica e Sociologia, Universita degli Studi di Firenze
The Netherlands:	Marcel van Dam, Geert Neelen, Anchrit Wille, Department of Public Administration, University of Leiden. Jaco Berveling, Dutch Transport Research Centre

Norway:	Harald Baldersheim, Morten Øgaard, Department of Political Science, Oslo University
Portugal:	Manuel da Silva e Costa, Joel Felizes, José P. Neves, Instituto de Ciências Sociais, Universidade do Minho
Spain:	Irene Delgado, Eliseo López, Lourdes López Nieto, Departamento de Ciencia Politica y de la Administración Universidad Nacional de Educacion a Distancia
Sweden:	Roger Haglund, Folke Johansson, Department of Political Science, University of Gothenburg
USA:	James Svara, Department of Political Science and Public Administration, North Carolina State University

References

Abramson, P. & R. Inglehart (1995). *Value change in global perspective*, Ann Arbor, MI: The University of Michigan Press.

Adams, G. & V.H. Ingersoll (1990). 'Painting over Old Works: The Culture of Organization in an Age of Technical Rationality', pp. 15-25, in B. Turner (ed.), *Organizational Symbolism*, Berlin: de Gruyter.

Adizes, I. (1979). *Lederens Faldgruber*, Odense: Børsens Forlag.

Albæk, E., L. Rose, L. Stromberg & K. Ståhlberg (1996). *Nordic Local Government*, Helsinki: The Association of Finnish Local Authorities.

Alexander, A. (1982). *Local government in Britain since reorganisation*, London: George Allen and Unwin.

Anderson, L. & M.N. Pedersen (1998). 'Rekruttering af Kommunale Chefer', *Politica*, vol. 30, no. 3, pp. 298-307.

Argyris, C. (1954). 'The Fusion of the Individual with the Organization', *American Sociological Review*, vol. 19. pp. 267-272.

Argyris, C. (1957). The Individual and Organization, some Problems of Mutual Adjustments, *Administrative Science Quarterly*, vol. 2, pp. 1-24.

Asquith, A. (1994). *Change management in local government: Strategic change agents and organisational ownership*, Ph.D.-thesis, Birmingham: University of Central England.

Asquith, A. & E. O'Halpin (1996a). *Continuity and change in public management: Irish local authority chief executives and their European counterparts in comparative perspective'*, paper presented to the conference on Management research in Ireland: The way forward.

Asquith, A. & E. O'Halpin (1996b). 'The Irish County and City Managers Association', pp. 50-56, in M. Goldsmith (ed.), *The associations of local government CEOs in Europe*, Odense: Odense University, School of Business and Economics.

Asquith, A. & E. O'Halpin (1997). 'The Irish Association of Local Government CEOs', pp. 72-77, in M. Goldsmith & P.E. Mouritzen (eds.), *Report of the 3rd U.Di.T.E. Congress*, Copenhagen: Kommunaldirektørforeningen i Danmark.

Asquith, A. (1997). 'Effecting change management in English local government', *Local Government Studies*, vol. 23,4, pp. 86-99.

Asquith, A. & E. O'Halpin (1998). 'The changing role of the Irish local government manager,' *Administration*, vol. 45,4, pp. 76-92.

Baier, V.E., J.G. March & H. Sætren (1986). 'Implementation and Ambiguity', *Scandinavian Journal of Management Studies*, vol. 2, no. 3-4, pp. 150-164.

Bakka, J.F. & E. Fivelsdal (1992). *Organisationsteori. Struktur, Kultur, Processer*, 2nd ed., Viborg: Nyt Nordisk Forlag.

Baldersheim, H. & M. Øgård (1999). *Vandringsmann med sordin. Flyttemønster og lederutfordringer blant norske rådmenn i komparativt perspektiv*, Forskningsrapport 4, Oslo: Institut for Statsvitenskap, Oslo University.

Barley, S.R. (1986). 'Technology as an occasion for structuring: evidence from observations of CT scanners and the social order of radiology departments', *Administrative Science Quaterly*, vol. 31, pp. 78-108.

Barry, N. (1991). 'Understanding the market', pp. 231-241, in M. Loney, R. Bocock, J. Clarke, A. Cochrane, P. Graham, & M. Wilson, *The state or the market*, 2nd ed., London: Sage.

Barthes, R. (1970). *Mytologier*, Copenhagen: Rhodos.

Bateson, G. (1972). *Steps to an Ecology of Mind*, New York: Ballantine.

Bedford Borough Council (1997). *Closer to the people – closer to the people's priorities*, Bedford: Bedford Borough Council.

Ben-Elia, N. (1996). 'Introduction', pp. 1-20, in N. Ben-Elia (ed.), *Stategic Changes and Organizational Reorientations in Local Government. A Cross-National Perspective*, London: MacMillan Press Ltd.

Bennis, W.G., K.D. Benne, R. Chin & K.E. Corey (1976). *The planning of change*, New York: Holt, Reinhart and Winston.

Bentzon, K.-H. (1988). *Fra vækst til omstilling – moderniseringen af den offentlige sektor*, Copenhagen: Nyt fra Samfundsvidenskaberne.

Berger, P.L. & T. Luckmann (1967). *The Social Construction of Reality. A Treatise in the Sociology og Knowledge*, New York: Doubleday & Company, Anchor Books.

Bergström, T. (1993). *Chefsbild i förändring. Platsannonsernas kommunale chefer 1982 och 1992*, paper presented at Nordiska Statsvetarkongressen, Oslo.

Berveling, J., M. van Dam, & G. Neelen (1997). *De Deugd in het Midden*, Delft: Eburon.

Bordum, A. (1997). *Diskursetikken og Det Etiske Regnskab. Principper for Ledelse mellem Magt og Konsensus*, unpublished Ph.D.-thesis, Institut for Ledelse, Politik og Filosofi, Copenhagen Business School.

Bouckaert, G., A. Hondeghem & R. Maes (1994). *De Overheidsmanager*, Leuven: VCOB.

Bourdieu, P. (1998). *Practical Reason. On the Theory of Action*, Cambridge, UK: Polity Press.

Bours, A. (1993). 'Management, tiers, size and amalgamations,' pp. 109-129, in R.J. Bennet (ed.), *Local government in the New Europe,* London: Belhaven Press.

Boyle, R., T. McNamara, M. Mulreaney & A. O'Keefe (1997). 'Review of developments in the public sector in 1996', *Administration*, vol. 44,4, pp. 3-44.

Boyton, J. (1986). *Job at the top. The chief executive in local government*, Harlow: Longman.

Brodbeck, F.C. et al. (2000). 'Cultural Variation of Leadership Prototypes across 22 European Countries', *Journal of Occupational and Organizational Psychology*, vol. 73, pp. 1-29.

Broms, H. & H. Gahmberg (1983). 'Communication to Self in Organizations and Cultures', *Administrative Science Quarterly*, vol. 28, pp. 482-495.

Brooke, R. (1991). 'The enabling authority'. *Public Administration,* vol. 69,4, pp. 525-532.

Brunsson, N. (1986). 'Organizing for Inconsistencies: On Organizational Conflict, Depression and Hypocrisy', *Scandinavian Journal of Management Studies*, May, pp. 165-185.

Brunsson, N. (1994). 'Politicization and 'company-ization' – on institutional affiliation and confusion in the organizational world', *Management Accounting Research*, vol. 5, pp. 323-335.

Bryman, A. (1992). *Charisma and Leadership in Organisations*, London: Sage Publications Ltd.

Burns, T. & G.M. Stalker (1961). *The management of innovation*, London: Tavistock.

Calas, M.S. & L. Smircich (1988). 'Reading Leadership as a Form of Cultural Analysis', pp. 201-226, in J. Hunt, B.R. Baliga, P. Dachler & C. Schriesheim (eds.), *Emerging Leadership Vistas*, Lexington: Lexington.

Calas, M.S. (1991). 'Voicing Seduction to Silence Leadership', *Organizational Studies*, vol. 12, no. 4, pp. 567-602.

Carlson, S. (1951/1991). *Executive behaviour. Reprinted with contributions by Henry Mintzberg and Rosemary Stewart*, Uppsala: Textgruppen i Uppsala AB.

Castles, F., R. Gerritsen & J. Vowles (eds.) (1996). *The great experiment: Labour parties and public policy transformation in Australia and New Zealand*, St. Leonards, NSW: Allen and Unwin.

Castoriadis, C. (1981). *Marxisme og revolutionær teori*, Copenhagen: Rhodos.

Certo, S.C. & J.P. Peter (1991). *Strategic management. Concepts and applications*, London: MacGraw Hill.

Clark, T. N. & V. Hoffmann-Martinot (1998). *The new political culture*, Boulder: Westview.

Clifford, J. & G.E. Marcus (eds.) (1986). *Writing Culture. The Poetics and Politics of Etnography*, Berkeley, Los Angeles, London: University of California Press.

Collins, N. (1987). *Local government managers at work*, Dublin: Institute of Public Administration.

Costa, M.S., J. Felizes, & J.P. Neves (1998). 'Portuguese chief administrative officers: between rationalization and political struggles', pp. 220-237, in K.K. Klausen & A. Magnier (eds.), *The Anonymous Leader – appointed CEOs in Western local government*, Odense: Odense University Press.

County and City Managers Association (1991). *County and city management 1929-1991: A retrospective*, Dublin: Institute of Public Adminstration.

Crozier, M. (1964). *The Bureaucratic Phenomenon*, Chicago: University of Chicago Press.

Czarniawska, B. & B. Joerges (1995). 'Winds of Organizational Change. How Ideas Change into Objects and Actions,' pp. 171-210, in S.B Bacharach, P. Gagliardi &

B. Mundell (eds.), *Research in the Sociology of Organizations*, Greenwich: JAI Press.

Czarniawska, B. & B. Joerges (1996). 'Travels of ideas', pp. 13-48, in B. Czarniawska & G. Sevon (eds.), *Translating Organizational Change*, Berlin: de Gruyter.

Czarniawska, B. & G. Sevon (eds.) (1996b). *Translating Organizational Change*, Berlin: de Gruyter.

Dahl, R. & E. Tufte (1973). *Size and democracy*, Stanford: Stanford University Press.

Dahler-Larsen, P. (1996). 'Udviklingen i kravene til danske kommunaldirektører de seneste tyve år belyst ved stillingsannoncer: en social konstruktion?' *Nordisk Administrativt Tidsskrift*, vol. 78, no. 2, pp. 119-142.

Davis, H. (1988). 'Local government under siege', *Public Administration*, vol. 66,1, pp. 91-101.

Dawson, D. & M. Saunders (1996). *Uses of Job Attributes as a Basis for Job Search and Application Decisions*, paper presented at Third Biennial International Conference on Advances in Management, Framingham, MA., USA.

Deleuze, G. & F. Guattari (1988). *A Thousand Plateaus: Capitalism and Schizophrenia*, London: Athlone Press.

DeHoog, R.H. & G.P. Whitaker (1990). 'Political Conflict or Professional Advancement: Alternative Explanations of City Manager Turnover', *Journal of Urban Affairs*, vol. 12, no. 4, pp. 361-377.

Delgado, I., L. Nieto & E. López (1998). 'Functions and Duties of Funcionarios Directivos Locales', pp. 238-252, in K.K. Klausen & A. Magnier (eds.), *The Anonymous Leader – appointed CEOs in Western local government*, Odense: Odense University Press.

Denzin, N.K. & Y.S. Lincoln (eds.) (1994). *Handbook of qualitative research*, Newbury Park, California: Sage.

Deresky, H. (1997). *International Management, Managing Across Borders and Cultures* 2nd ed., Reading: Addison-Wesley.

DiMaggio, P.J. & W.D. Powell (1991). 'Introduction', pp. 1-140, in P.J. DiMaggio & W.D. Powell (eds.). *The New Institutionalism in Organizational Analysis*, Chicago: The University of Chicago Press.

DiMaggio, P.J. & W.D. Powell (1991). 'The Iron Cage Revisited: Institutional Isomorphism and Collective Rationality in Organizational Fields', pp. 63-82 in P.J. DiMaggio & W.D. Powell (eds.). *The New Institutionalism in Organizational Analysis*, Chicago: The University of Chicago Press.

DJØF (1996). (*Amts*)*kommunale topchefers ansættelsestryghed*. Betænkning fra Udvalget om (amts)kommunale topchefers ansættelsestryghed. [Committee Report on County and Local Government CEOs' Job Security].

Dunleavy, P. & C. Hood. (1994). 'From old Administration to New Public management', *Public Money and Management,* July-Sept., pp. 9-16.

Ejersbo, N. (1996). *Den kommunale forvaltning under omstilling. En organisations-*

teoretisk analyse af effekterne af forvaltningsændringer ud fra et ledelsesperspektiv, Ph.D.-thesis, Odense: The Faculty of Social Sciences, Odense University.

Ejersbo, N., M.B. Hansen & P.E. Mouritzen (1998). 'The Danish Local government CEO: From Town Clerk to City Manager', pp. 97-112, in Kurt Klaudi Klausen & Annick Magnier, *The Anonymous Leader. Appointed CEOs in Western Local Government*, Odense: Odense University Press.

Elcock, H. (1994). *Local government. Policy and management in local authorities*, London: Routledge.

Eliassen, K.A. & J. Kooiman (eds.) (1993). *Managing public organizations. Lessons from contemporary European experience*, London: Sage.

Espejo, R. (1989). 'The VSM revisited', pp. 77-100, in R. Espejo & R. Harnden (eds.), *The Viable System Model: Interpretations and Applications of Stafford Beers VSM*, Chichester: Wiley.

Espejo, R. & R. Harnden (1989). *The Viable System Model: Interpretations and applications of Stafford Beers VSM*, Chichester: Wiley.

Etzioni, A. (1972). *Moderne organisationer*, Copenhagen: Reitzel.

Eulau, H. (1969). *Micro-macro Political Analysis*, Chicago: Aldine.

Ferlie, E., L. Ashburner, L. Fitzgerald & A. Pettigrew (1996). *The new public management in action*, Oxford: Oxford University Press.

Flynn, N. & F. Strehl (1996). 'Introduction', pp. 1-22, in N. Flynn & F. Strehl (ed.), *Public sector management in Europe*, Hertfordshire: Prentice Hall, Harvester Wheatsheaf.

Flynn, N. & F. Strehl (eds.) (1996). *Public sector management in Europe*, Hemel Hempstead: Prentice Hall.

Flynn, N. (1997). *Public Sector Management*. 3rd ed., New York: Harvester Wheatsheaf.

Foucault, M. (1979). *Discipline and Punish*, Harmondsworth: Penguin.

Foucault, M. (1980). *Power/Knowledge. Selected Interviews and Other Writings 1972-77 by Michel Foucault*. Edited by Colin Gordon, New York: Harvester Wheatsheaf.

Foucault, M. (1983). 'Afterword: the subject and power', pp. 208-228, in H.L. Dreyfus & P. Rabinow, *Michel Foucault: Beyond Structuralism and Hermeneutics*, 2nd ed., Chicago: University of Chicago Press.

Foucault, M. (1971). 'Orders of Discourse. Technologies of the Self', *Social Science Information*, vol. 10:2, pp. 7-30.

Friedland, R. & R.R. Alford (1991). 'Bringing Society Back In: Symbols, Practices and Institutional Contradictions', pp. 232-263, in Walter D. Powell & Paul J. DiMaggio, *The New Institutionalism in Organizational Analysis,* Chicago: The University of Chicago Press.

Gamberucci, M. & A. Magnier (1998). 'Italian Local Democracy in Search of a New Administrative Leadership', pp. 204-219, in K.K. Klausen & A. Magnier (eds.), *The Anonymous Leader – appointed CEOs in Western local government,* Odense: Odense University Press.

Gargan, J.J. (ed.) (1996). *Handbook of local government administration*, New York: Marcel Dekker.

Geertz, C. (1973). 'Thick Description: Toward an Interpretive Theory of Culture', *The Interpretation of Cultures. Selected Essays*, pp. 3-30, New York: Harper Collins, Basic Books.

Gerritsen, R. & M. Whyard (1998). 'The Challenge of Constant Change: The Australian Local Government CEO', pp. 31-48, in K.K. Klausen & A. Magnier (eds.), *The Anonymous Leader – appointed CEOs in Western local government,* Odense: Odense University Press.

Giddens, A. (1984). *The Constitution of Society. Outline of the Theory of Structuration*, Berkeley: University of California Press.

Giddens, A. (1993). *New Rules of Sociological Method. A Positive Critique of Interpretive Sociologies*, 2nd ed., Stanford, California: Stanford University Press.

Goffman, E. (1959). *The Presentation of Self in Everyday Life*, New York: Anchor Books.

Goffman, E. (1974). *Frame Analysis. An Essay on the Organization of Experience*, Boston: Northeastern University Press.

Goffman, E. (1983). 'The interaction order', *American Sociological Review*, vol. 48, February, pp. 1-17.

Goldsmith, M. (1995). 'Autonomy and city limits', pp. 228-252, in D. Judge, G. Stoker, & H. Wolman (eds.), *Theories of Urban Politics*, London: Sage.

Goldsmith, M. (1996). 'Normative Theories of Local Government: A European Comparison', pp. 174-192, in D. King & G. Stoker (eds.), *Rethinking Local Democracy*, London: Macmillan Press.

Goldsmith, M. & P.E. Mouritzen (eds.) (1997). *The Udite Leadership Study*, Copenhagen: Kommunaldirektørforeningen i Danmark.

Goldsmith, M. & J. Tonge (1998) 'Local Authority Chief Executives – the British Case', pp. 49-63, in K.K. Klausen & A. Magnier (eds.), *The Anonymous Leader – appointed CEOs in Western local government,* Odense: Odense University Press.

Goodsell, C. (1985). *The case for bureaucracy*, Chatham: Chatham House.

Gosling, P. (1997). 'Kiwis go to town', *The Independent Tabloid,* 23.01.97, p. 23.

Gouldner, A. (1954). *Patterns of Industrial Bureaucracy*, New York: Collier MacMillan.

Grémion, P. (1976). *Le Pouvoir Périphérique: bureaucrates et notables dans le système politique francais*, Paris: Seuil.

Habermas, J. (1995). *Postmetaphysical Thinking*, Cambridge: Polity Press.

Haglund, R. (1998). 'Turbulence as a Way of Life: The Swedish Municipal CEO', pp. 140-158, in K.K. Klausen & A. Magnier (eds.), *The Anonymous Leader – appointed CEOs in Western local government,* Odense: Odense University Press.

Hales, C.P. (1986). 'What do Managers Do? A Critical Review of the Evidence', *Management Studies*, vol. 23, no. 1, pp. 88-115.

Hales, C.P. (1993). *Managing through organisation. The management process, forms of organisation and the work of managers*, London: Routledge.

Hansen, M.B. (1997). *Kommunaldirektøren – Marionet og dirigent. En Organisationssociologisk undersøgelse af struktureringen af kommunaldirektørens arbejde med udgangspunkt i et aktør-struktur perspektiv*, Ph.D.-thesis, Odense: Faculty of Social Sciences, University of Southern Denmark.

Hansen, M.B. (1998). 'Chefgruppemødet – fra informationsformidling til kollektiv ledelse?', *Politica,* vol. 30, no. 3, pp. 270-284.

Harmon, M.M. & R.T. Mayer (1986). *Organization Theory for Public Administration*, Glenview, Illinois: Scott, Foresman and Company.

Harzing, A.W. & G. Hofstede (1996). 'Planned Change in Organizations: The Influence of National Culture', *Research on the Sociology of Organizations*, vol. 14, pp. 297-340.

Headrick, T.E. (1962). *The town clerk in English local government*, London: Allen and Unwin.

Herzberg, F., B. Mausner & B. Snyderman (1959). *Work and Motivation*, New York: Wiley.

Hesse, J.J. & L.J. Sharpe (1991). 'Local Government in International Perspective – some comparative observations', pp. 603-621, in J. Hesse. & L.J. Sharpe (eds.), *Local Government and Urban Affairs in International Perspective*, Baden-Baden: Nomos Verlagsgesellschaft.

Hesselbein, F., M. Goldsmith & R. Beckhard (eds.) (1997a). *The leader of the future*, San Francisco: Jossey Bass.

Hesselbein, F., M. Goldsmith, & R. Beckhard (eds.) (1997b). *The organisation of the future*, San Francisco: Jossey Bass.

Hoffmann-Martinot, V. & D. Kjellberg (1996). *Centraliser en France et en Norvege*, Paris: Pedone.

Hofstede, G. (1972). 'The Color of Collars, Occupational Differences in Work Goals', *Columbia Journal of World Business*, vol. 7,5, pp. 72-80.

Hofstede, G. (1980/84). *Culture's Consequences, International Differences in Work-Related Values*, Beverly Hills: Sage Publications.

Hofstede, G. (1984). 'The Cultural Relativity of the Quality of Life Concept'. *Academy of Management Review*, vol. 9, pp. 389-398.

Hofstede, G. (1989). *Sozialisation am Arbeitsplatz aus Kulturvergleichender Sicht*, Ferdinand Enke Verlag.

Hofstede, G. (1994a). *Cultures and Organizations: Software of the Mind. Intercultural Cooperation and its Importance for Survival*, London: McGraw-Hill.

Hofstede, G. (1994b). *Uncommon Sense About Organizations, Cases, Studies, and Field Observations*, London: Sage Publications.

Hofstede, G. (1994c). *Values Survey Module 1994*, Maastricht: Institute for Research on Intercultural Cooperation, University of Limburg.

Hofstede, G. (1996). A Hopscotch Hike, *Management Laureats*, vol. 4, pp. 85-122.

Hofstede, G., M.H. Bond & C.-L. Luk (1993). 'Individual Perceptions of Organizational Cultures: A Methodological Treatise on Levels of Analysis', *Organization Studies*, vol. 14, no. 4, pp. 483-503.

Holsti, O. (1969). *Content Analysis for the Social Sciences and Humanities*, Reading, Mass.: Addison-Wesley.

Hood, C. (1991). 'A public management for all seasons?' *Public Administration*, vol. 69, no. Spring 1991, pp. 3-19.

Hoppe, M.H. (1990). *A Comparative Study of Country Elites: International Differences in Work-Related Values and Learning and their Implications for International Management Training and Development,* unpublished Ph.D.-thesis, University of North Carolina at Chapel Hill.

Hoppe, M.H. (1992). *The Effects of National Culture on the Theory and Practice of Managing R&D Professional Abroad*, unpublished paper presented at the conference 'Managing R & D Professionals Internationally', Manchester: Manchester Business School, R & D Research Unit, 6-8 July.

Hughes, E.C. (1951). 'Career and Office', pp. 95-102, in R. Dubin (ed.), *Human Relations in Administration*, The Sociology of Organization: Prentice Hall.

Hughes, O. E. (1994). *Public management and administration*, Basingstoke: Macmillan.

Hunt, J., B.R. Baliga, P. Dachler & C. Schriesheim (eds.) (1988). *Emerging Leadership Vistas*, Lexington: Lexington.

Hutton, W. (1995). *The state we're in*, London: Jonathan Cape.

Hutton, W. (1997a). *The state to come*, London: Jonathan Cape.

Hutton, W. (1997b). *Stakeholding and its critics*, London: Institute of Economic Affairs.

Inglehart, R. (1977). *The silent revolution*, Princeton, NJ.: Princeton University Press.

Inglehart, R. (1991). *Culture shock*, Princeton: NJ: University of Princeton Press.

Isaac-Henry, K. & C. Painter (1991a). 'The management challenge in local government – emerging themes and trends', *Local Government Studies*, vol. 17,3, pp. 69-90.

Isaac-Henry, K. & C. Painter (1991b). 'Organisational response to environmental turbulence: the management of change in English local government', *The International Journal of Public Sector Management*, vol. 4,4, pp. 5-20.

Isaac-Henry, K. (1997). 'Development and change in the public sector', pp. 1-25, in K. Issac-Henry, C. Painter & C. Barnes (eds.), *Management in the public sector. Challenge and change*, 2nd ed., London: Thompson International Business Press.

Issac-Henry, K., C. Painter, & C. Barnes (eds.) (1997). *Management in the public sector. Challenge and change*, London: Thompson International Business Press.

Jablin, F. (1987). 'Organizational Entry, Assimilation, and Exit', pp. 679-727, in F. Jablin, *Handbook og Organizational Communication. An interdisciplinary Perspective*, Newbury Park, California: Sage.

Jackson, T. (1993). *Organizational Behavior in International Management*, Oxford: Butterford-Heinemann.

Jepperson, R. L. (1991). 'Institutions, Institutional Effects, and Institutionalization', pp. 143-163, in W. Powell & P. DiMaggio (eds.), *The New Institutionalism in Organizational Analysis*, Chicago: The University of Chicago Press.

Jepperson, R. & J. Meyer (1991). 'The Public Order and the Construction of Formal Organizations', pp. 204-231, in W. Powell & P. DiMaggio (eds.), *The New Institutionalism in Organizational Analysis,* Chicago and London: The University of Chicago Press.

Johnson, E. (1997). 'The challenge to the public sector: changing politics and ideologies', pp. 26-44, in K. Issac-Henry, C. Painter & C. Barnes, *Management in the Public Sector. Challenge and Change*, London: Thompson International Business Press.

Jones, G. & T. Travers (1996). 'Central government perceptions of local government', pp. 84-105, in L. Pratchett & D. Wilson (eds.), *Local democracy and local government,* Houndmills: Macmillan.

Jordan, G. & N. Ashford (eds.) (1993). *Public policy and the impact of the New Right*, London: Pinter.

Jørgensen, T.B. & P. Melander (eds.) (1992). *Livet i offentlige organisationer. Institutionsdrift i spændingsfelt mellem stat, profession og marked*, Charlottenlund: Jurist- og Økonomforbundets Forlag.

Jørgensen, T.B. & P.E. Mouritzen (1993). *Udgiftspolitik og budgetlægning*, Systime: Herning.

Jørgensen, T.B., H. Foss Hansen, M. Antonsen & P. Melander (1996). 'Offentlige organisationer mellem politik og produktion,' *Nordisk Administrativt Tidsskrift,* vol. 1,77, pp. 5-36.

Kanter, R.M. (1990). *When giants learn to dance*, London: Unwin Paperbacks.

Kanungo, R.N. & R. W. Wright (1983). 'A Cross-Cultural Comparative Study of Managerial Job Attitudes', *Journal of International Business Studies*, vol. 14, pp. 115-129.

Keenan, P. (1993). 'Westminster seeks supermarket standards in service provision', *Local Government Chronicle*, 5.2.93, p. 10.

Kerley, R. (1994). *Managing in local government*, Basingstoke: Macmillan.

King, C. & C. Stivers (1998). *Government is us. Public Administration in an Anti-Government era*, London: Sage.

King, D. & G. Stoker (1996). *Rethinking local democracy*, Houndmills: Macmillan.

Klausen, K.K. & A. Magnier (eds.) (1998). *The Anonymous Leader – appointed CEOs in Western local government*, Odense: Odense University Press.

Kuylaars, A.M. (1951). *Werk en leven van de industriele loonarbeide, als object van een sociale ondernemingspolitiek*, Leiden: Stenfert Kroese.

Leach, S., J. Stewart, & K. Walsh (1994). *The changing organisation and management of local government*, Basingstoke: Macmillan.

Leach, S. & C. Collinge (1998). *Strategic planning and management in local government*, London: Pitman Publishing.

Levitt, B. & J. March (1988). 'Organizational Learning', *Annual Review of Sociology*, vol. 14, pp. 319-336.

Lijphart, A. (1971). 'Comparative Politics and the Comparative Method', *American Political Science Review*, LXV, pp. 682-93.

Lijphart, A. (1975). 'The Comparable-Cases Strategy in Comparative Research', *Comparative Political Studies*, vol. 8, no. 2, pp. 158-177.

Loney, M., R. Bocock, J. Clarke, A. Cochrane, P. Graham & M. Wilson (eds.) (1991). *The state or the market*, London: Sage.

Lowenduski, J. (1986). *Women and European politics*, Sussex: Wheatsheaf Books.

Lowenduski, J. & P. Norris (eds.) (1993). *Gender and party politics*, London: Sage.

Mackie, T. & D. Marsh (1995). 'The Comparative Method', pp. 173-188, in D. Marsh & G. Stoker (eds.), *Theory and Methods in Political Science,* London: MacMillan Press.

Maes, R. (1997). 'Het profiel van de lokale politiek', *Res Publica*, vol. 39,1, p. 10.

Magnier, Annick (1997). *La leadership amministrativa nel comune italiano*, Bologna: Editrice Compositori.

March, J.G. & J.P. Olsen (1984). 'The New Institutionalism: Organizational Factors in Political Life', *American Political Science Review*, vol. 78, pp. 734-749.

March, J.G. & J.P. Olsen (1989). *Rediscovering Institutions: The Organizational Basis of Politics*, New York: The Free Press.

March, J.G. (1991). 'Organizational Consultants and Organizational Research', *Journal of Applied Communication Research*, June, pp. 20-31.

March, J.G. & J.P. Olsen (1995). *Democratic Governance*, New York: The Free Press.

March, J.G. (1995). *Fornuft og Forandring. Ledelse i en verden beriget med uklarhed*, Copenhagen: Samfundslitteratur.

Martinko, M.J. & W.L. Gardner. (1985). 'Beyond Structured Observation: Methodological Issues and New Directions', *Academy of Management Review*, vol. 10, no. 4, pp. 676-695.

Maslow, A. H. (1954). *Motivation and Personality*, New York: Harper & Row.

McLean, I. (1987). *Public choice*, Oxford: Basil Blackwell.

Meindl, J. R., S.B. Ehrlich, & J.M. Dukerich. (1985). 'The Romance of Leadership', *Administrative Science Quarterly*, vol. 30, pp. 78-102.

Merton, R.K. (1949). *Social theory and Social Structure*, New York: Free Press.

Meyer, J. & B. Rowan (1977). 'Formal Structure as Myth and Ceremony', *American Journal of Sociology,* vol. 83, pp. 340-363.

Meyer, J.W., J. Boli & G. Thomas (1987). 'Ontology and Rationalization in the Western Cultural Account', pp. 9-27, in W.R. Scott, J.W. Meyer & Associates (eds.), *Institutional Environments and Organizations. Structural Complexity and Individualism*, Thousand Oaks: Sage Publications.

Meyer, J.W., W.R. Scott, & Associates (1994). *Institutional Environments and Organizations. Structural Complexity and Individualism*, Thousand Oaks: Sage Publications.

Mintzberg, H. (1973). *The Nature of Managerial Work*, London: Prentice-Hall.

Mintzberg, H. (1983). *Structure in Fives: Designing Effective Organizations*, Englewood Cliffs: Prentice-Hall.
Mintzberg, H. (1991). 'Managerial Work: Forty Years Later', pp. 97-119, in S. Carlson (ed.), *Executive behaviour. Reprinted with contributions by Henry Mintzberg and Rosemary Stewart*, Stockholm: Almqvist & Wiksell.
Morgan, G. (1986). *Images of Organization*, Newbury Park: Sage.
Morgan, G. (1988). *Riding the waves of change*, San Francisco: Jossey Bass.
Morphett, J. (1993). *The role of Chief Executives in local government*, Harlow: Longmann.
Morris, R. & R. Paine (1995). *Will you manage? The needs of local authority chief executives*, Hemel Hempstead: ICSA Publishing.
Mouzelis, N. (1995). *Sociological Theory. What Went Wrong? Diagnosis and Remedies*, London: Routledge.
Newman, J. (1994). 'Beyond the vision: Cultural change in the public sector', *Public Money and Management*, vol. 14,2, pp. 59-64.
Newman, J. (1996). *Shaping organisational cultures in local government*, London: Pitman Publishing.
Nichols, C.T. (ed.) (1994). *Urban innovation*, Thousand Oaks, California: Sage.
Nielsen, J.F. (1985). *Kommunal organisering: en undersøgelse af bindinger, konflikter og ændringer i kommunale forvaltninger*, Århus: Politica
Niskanen, W. (1973). *Bureaucracy: Servant or master?*, London: Institute of Economic Affairs.
Niskanen, W. A. (1971). *Bureaucracy and Representative Government*, Chicago: Aldine-Atherton.
Norton, A. (1991). *The Role of the Chief Executive in English Local Government*, Birmingham: University of Birmingham Institute of Local Government Studies.
Norton, A. (1994). *International Handbook of Local and Regional Government. A comparative analysis of advanced democracies*, Aldershot: Edward Elgar.
O'Halpin, E. (1991). 'The origins of county and city management', pp. 1-20, in *County and City Managers Association, County and City Management 1929-1991: A retrospective*, Dublin: Institute of Public Administration.
Olsen, J.P. (1978). *Politisk Oganisering*, Bergen: Universitetsforlaget.
OECD (1996). *National Accounts*, Paris.
Osborne, D. & T. Gaebler (1992). *Reinventing Government. How the Entrepreneurial Spirit is Transforming the Public Sector*, Reading: Addison-Wesley.
Page, E. (1990). 'The Political Origins of Self-Government and Bureaucracy: Otto Hintze's Conceptual Map of Europe', *Political Studies*, vol. 38, no. 1, pp. 39-55.
Painter, C. (1994). 'Public service reform: Reinventing or abandoning government', *Political Quarterly*, vol. 65,3, pp. 242-262.
Painter, C. (1997). 'Managing change in the public sector', pp. 45-72, in K. Issac-Henry, C. Painter & C. Barnes (eds.), *Management in the public sector. Challenge and change*, London: Thompson International Business Press.

Palumbo, D.J. (ed.) (1985). *The politics of program evaluation*, Newbury Park, California: Sage Publications.

Perrow, C. (1972). *Complex Organizations: a critical essay*, Illinois: Scott Foresman.

Peters, B.G. (1995). *The Politics of Bureaucracy*, New York: Longman Publishers.

Peters, B.G. (1997). 'Shouldn't row, can't steer: What's a Government to do?' *Public Policy and Administration*, vol. 12,2, pp. 51-61.

Peters, T.J. (1992). *Liberation Management*, London: Macmillan.

Plees, Y. & T. Laurent (1998). 'The Belgian Municipal Secretary: A Manager for the Municipalities?', pp. 173-187, in K.K. Klausen & A. Magnier (eds.), *The Anonymous Leader – appointed CEOs in Western local government,* Odense: Odense University Press.

Politt, C. (1993). *Managerialism and the public services*, Oxford: Basil Blackwell.

Politt, C. (1995). 'Justification by Works or by Faith? Evaluating the New Public Management', *Evaluation*, vol. 1, no. 2, pp. 133-154.

Posner, B.Z. & J.M. Munson (1979). 'The Impact of Subordinate-Supervisor Value Consensus', *Akron Business & Economic Review (ABE)*, vol. 10, pp. 37-40.

Powell, W.D. & DiMaggio (eds.) (1991). *The New Institutionalism in Organizational Analysis*, Chicago: The University of Chicago Press.

Przeworski, A. & H. Teune (1970). *The Logic of Comparative Social Inquiry*, New York, London, Toronto, Sydney: Wiley-Interscience.

Pugh, D.S., B. Hickson & C.R. Hinnings (1969). 'The Context of Organization Structure', *Administrative Science Quarterly*, vol. 14,1, pp. 91-114.

Putnam, R. (1976). *The comparative study of political elites*, Englewood Cliff, NJ: Prentice Hall.

Quirk, B. (1991). 'At the open end of change', *Local Government Chronicle*, vol. 22.02.91, pp. 15-15.

Ragin, C.C. (1994). *Constructing Social Research: The Unity and Diversity of Method*, Newbury Park: Pine Forgess Press.

Ranson, S. & J. Stewart (1994). *Management for the public domain*, Basingstoke: Macmillan.

Reed, M. (1985). *Redirections in Organizational Analysis*. London: Tavistock Publications.

Ridley, N. (1988). *The local right: enabling not providing*, London: Centre for Policy Studies.

Riiskjær, E. (1982). *Kommunale Forvaltningschefer: en forskningsrapport om kommunale forvaltningschefer – ledelsesrammer, rekrutteringsbaggrund og holdninger*, Århus: Politica.

Roche, D. (1982). *Local government in Ireland*, Dublin: Institute of Public Administration.

Rokkan, S., S. Verba, J. Viet & E. Almasy (1969). *Comparative Survey Analysis*, The Hague: Mouton.

Ronen, S. & O. Shenkar (1985). 'Clustering Countries on Attitudinal Dimensions: a Review and Synthesis', *Academy of Management Review*, vol. 27, pp. 230-264.

Ronen, S. (1986). *Comparative and Multinational Management*, New York: Wiley and Sons.

Rouse, J. (1997). 'Resource and performance management in public service organisations', pp. 73-104, in K. Issac-Henry, C. Painter & C. Barnes (eds), *Management in the public sector. Challenge and change,* London: Thompson International Business Press.

Rustow, D. A. (1968). 'Modernization and Comparative Politics: Prospects in Research and Theory', *Comparative Politics,* vol. 1, pp. 45-47.

Røvik, K.-A. (1992). *Den syke stat: Myter og moter i omstillingsarbeidet*, Oslo: The Norwegian University Press.

Sabin, P. (1990). 'The role of the chief executive in Kent County Council', *Local Government Policy Making*, vol. 17,1, pp. 24-28.

Sahlins, M. (1976). *Culture and Practical Reason*, Chicago: Aldine.

Sandberg, S. (1998). 'The Strong CEOs of Finland', pp. 113-127, in K.K. Klausen & A. Magnier (eds.), *The Anonymous Leader – appointed CEOs in Western local government,* Odense: Odense University Press.

Scott, W.R. (1995). *Institutions and Organizations*, Thousand Oaks: Sage Publications

Self, P. (1993). *Government by the market*, Basingstoke: Macmillan.

Selznick, P. (1949). *TVA and the Grass Roots*, Berkeley: University of California Press.

Sevon, G. (1996). 'Organizational Imitation in Identity Transformation', pp. 49-68, in B. Czarniawska & G. Sevon (eds.), *Translating Organizational Change*, Berlin: de Gruyter.

Sharpe, L.J. (1993). *The Rise of the Meso Government in Europe*, London: Sage.

Sharpe, L.J. (1996). 'The Modernization of Local Government in the Modern Democratic State', pp. 15-33, in P. Bogason (ed.), *New Modes of Local Organising: local government fragmentation in Scandinavia*, Commack: Nova Sciences.

Skelcher, C. (1992). *Managing for service quality*, Harlow: Longman.

Smith, P.B., S. Dugan & F. Trompenaas (1996). 'National Culture and the Values of Organizational Employees', *Journal of Work and Organizational Psychology*, vol. 27, pp. 230-264.

Spenner, K.I., L.B. Otto & V.R.A. Call (1982). *Career Lines and Careers*, Lexington: Lexington Books.

Spilerman, S. (1977). 'Careers, Labor Market Structure, and Socioeconomic Achievement', *American Journal of Sociology*, vol. 83, pp. 550-570.

Stake, R.E. (1994). 'Case Studies', pp. 236-247, in N. Denzin & Y. Lincoln (eds.), *Handbook of Qualitative Research*, Thousand Oaks: Sage.

Stewart, J. & M. Clarke. (1987). 'The public service orientation: Issues and dilemmas', *Public Administration*, vol. 65,2, pp. 161-177.

Stewart, J. (1988). *Understanding the management of local government*, Harlow: Longman.

Stewart, J. & G. Stoker (1995). *Local Government in the Nineties*, Macmillan: London.

Stewart, R. (1982). *Choices for the manager. A guide to managerial work and behaviour*, London: McGraw-Hill Book Company (UK) Limited.

Stewart, R. (1989). 'Studies of Managerial Jobs and Behaviour: The Ways Forward', *Journal of Management Studies*, vol. 26, no.1, pp. 1-10.

Stewart, R. & N. Fondas (1994). 'Enactment in Managerial Jobs: A Role Analysis', *Journal of Management Studies*, vol. 31, no.1, pp. 83-103.

Stigler, G. (1975). *The citizen and the state*, Chicago: University of Chicago Press.

Stillman II, R.J. (1977). 'The City Manager: Professional helping hand, or political hired hand', *Public Administration Review*, 37 (November/December), pp. 659-670.

Strand, T. (1993). 'Bureaucrats and Other Manager Roles in Transition', pp. 157-173, in K.A. Eliassen, J. Kooiman (eds.), *Managing Public Organizations*, London: Sage.

Strang, D. & J.W. Meyer (1994). 'Institutional Conditions for Diffusion', pp. 100-112, in W.R. Scott, J.W. Meyer & Associates (eds.), *Institutional Environments and Organizations. Structural Complexity and Individualism*, Thousand Oaks: Sage.

Svara, J. H. (1996). 'Professional administration (and representative governance) in the Council-Manager City', pp. 349-386, in J.J. Gargan (ed.), *Handbook of local government administration*, New York: Marcel Dekker.

Svara, J. (1998). 'United States of America: Similarity Within Diversity', pp. 78-96, in K.K. Klausen & A. Magnier (eds.), *The Anonymous Leader – appointed CEOs in Western local government*, Odense: Odense University Press.

Svara, J. & P.E. Mouritzen (2001): *Leadership at the Apex. Politicians and Administrators in Western Local Governments*, Pittsburgh: Pittsburgh University Press.

Søndergaard, M. (1994). 'Research Note: Hofstede's Consequences: A Study of Reviews, Citations and Replications', *Organization Studies*, vol. 15,3, pp. 447-456.

Terpstra, D.E. (1980). 'Leadership and Motivation: A Case for Conceptual and Empirical Cross-Fertilization', *Akron Business & Economic Review (ABE)*, vol. 11, pp. 51-55.

Thoenig, J.-C. & K. Burlen (1998). 'The Asymmetric Interdependence Between two Powerful Actors: The CEO and the Mayor in French Cities', pp. 183-203, in K.K. Klausen & A. Magnier (eds.), *The Anonymous Leader – appointed CEOs in Western local government*, Odense: Odense University Press.

Tompkins, P.K. (1987). 'Translating Organizational Theory: Symbolism over Substance', pp. 70-96, in F.M. Jablin (ed.), *Handbook of Organizational Communication*, Newbury Park: Sage.

Ungerson, B. (1975). 'Introduction: The Scientific Method in Selection', pp. 3-10, in B. Ungerson (ed.), *Recruitment Handbook* 2nd ed., Guildford: Gower Press.

Walsh, K. (1995). *Public Services and Market mechanisms*, Macmillan: London.

Waterman, R.H. (1988). *The renewal factor*, London: Bantam.

Watson, T.J. (1994). *In search of management. Culture, chaos and control in managerial work*, London: Routledge.

Watt, S. (1997). 'Competition voodoo they do down under', *Local Government Chronicle*, 12.09.97, pp. 16-17.

Weber, M. (1946). *From Max Weber: Essays in Sociology*, New York: Oxford University Press.

Weber, Max (1971). *Makt og byråkrati: Essays om politikk og klasse, samfunnsforskning og verdier*, Oslo: Gyldendal Norsk Forlag.

Weick, K. (1976). 'Educational Organizations as Loosely Coupled Systems', *Administrative Science Quarterly*, vol. 21,1, pp. 1-19.

Whittington, R. (1992). 'Putting Giddens into Action: Social Systems and Managerial Agency', *Journal of Management Studies,* vol. 29, no. 6, November, pp. 693-712.

Wildawsky, A. (1974). *The Politics of the Budgetary Process*, Boston: Little, Brown & Co.

Willmott, H. (1987). 'Studying Managerial Work: A Critique and a Proposal', *Journal of Management Studies*, vol. 24, no. 3, pp. 249-270.

Wilson, D. & C. Game (1998). *Local government in the United Kingdom*, 2nd ed., Basingstoke: Macmillan.

Wise, L.R. (1996). 'Internal Labour Markets', pp. 100-118, in H.A.G.M. Bekke, J.L. Perry & T.A.J. Toonen (eds.), *Civil Service Systems in Comparative Perspective*, Bloomington: Indiana University Press.

Woodward, J. (1965). *Industrial Organization Theory and Practise*, London: Oxford University Press.

Yukl, G. (1994). *Leadership in Organizations*, 3rd ed., Englewood Cliffs: Prentice Hall.